NAB EXECUTIVE TECHNOLOGY BRIEFINGS

Expanding a Digital Content Management System

For the Growing Digital Media Enterprise

Magan H. Arthur

National Association of
NAB
BROADCASTERS®

AMSTERDAM • BOSTON • HEIDELBERG • LONDON
NEW YORK • OXFORD • PARIS • SAN DIEGO
SAN FRANCISCO • SINGAPORE • SYDNEY • TOKYO
Focal Press Is an Imprint of Elsevier

Focal
Press

Acquisitions Editor:	Angelina Ward
Project Manager:	Brandy Lilly
Marketing Manager	Christine Degon Veroulis
Development Editor:	Beth Millett
Assistant Editor:	Rachel Epstein
Cover Design:	Frances Baca Design
Interior Design:	Frances Baca Design
Composition and Illustration:	Umbrella Graphics
Indexer:	borregopublishing.com

Focal Press is an imprint of Elsevier
30 Corporate Drive, Suite 400, Burlington, MA 01803, USA
Linacre House, Jordan Hill, Oxford OX2 8DP, UK

∞ Recognizing the importance of preserving what has been written, Elsevier prints its books on acid-free paper whenever possible.

Library of Congress Application Submitted Cataloging-in-Publication Data

British Library Cataloguing-in-Publication Data
A catalogue record for this book is available from the British Library.

ISBN 13: 978-0-240-80794-2

For information on all Focal Press publications
visit our website at www.books.elsevier.com

Transferred to digital printing in 2009.

Working together to grow
libraries in developing countries
www.elsevier.com | www.bookaid.org | www.sabre.org

ELSEVIER   BOOK AID International   Sabre Foundation

*To Rachel, Lola, Julia and Dolano for your love
that makes me enjoy my life and work so deeply.*
—Magan Arthur

Acknowledgements

I would like to thank the following individuals and companies for their support and encouragement in writing this book: Yair Dembinsky, CKO at Rafael Ltd.; Kerry Barner and the people at Henry Stewart (J-DAM); George Song and his company, 55 Minutes; Chester Chen, Director of Development at ClearStory Systems; John Fox, founder and former CTO of WebWare; Carlos Montalvo, CMO at Northplains; Tony Byrne at CMS Watch; Paola Di Maio; Mark Well, CTO at TranTech; Shuli Goodman; Scott Smith; Jeremy Bancroft, Broadcast Consultant; Blue Order; Digimarc; Tamra Yoder, Strategic Group Leader at Harcourt Inc.; Joel Warwick, Content Management Consultant, Corbis, and Gil Weigand, SVP Digital Strategy, CanWest MediaWorks. A special thank you goes to Hannah Pirone, who has helped me with editing and structuring the book.

Author Biography

Magan Arthur, a technology veteran, is a world-leading expert on digital content management. Mr. Arthur worked in different roles for WebWare (now ClearStory Systems), the legendary pioneer of digital asset management on web-based platforms, before founding the consulting company ACG (Arthur Consulting Group). He is currently the principal solutions consultant for Infosys Technologies Ltd. Media and Entertainment Practice. He led the implementations of dozens of large-scale digital asset management systems at Global 1000 companies and has worked with universities in Europe and the U.S. on knowledge management and e-learning solutions. Today, he is advising media and entertainment companies on digital strategy and the future of the digital media enterprise. He studied at the Friedrich Wilhelm's University in Bonn, Germany, as well as at the Humaniversity in Egmond an Zee, Netherlands.

Contents

Introduction xi

1   **Defining the Starting Point and Direction of the Expansion** 1

2   **Preparing the Organization for Expansion** 13

3   **Definition of Technologies and Products** 21

4   **System Definition Recommendations and Advanced Concepts** 33

5   **Digital Rights Management, Authentication, and Compliance** 47

6   **Building the Business Case for a System Expansion** 57

7   **ROI Models** 67

8   **Expanding the System Hardware and Software** 83

9   **Integration** 97

10 **Advanced Taxonomy (Classification System)** 107

11 **Metadata** 121

    Appendix 135

    Index 145

Introduction

The concept of the digital media enterprise was developed by the media and entertainment practice at Infosys Technologies. Its vision is a new approach to the technologies and practices that drive the media and entertainment industry. The author has been a key architect of this concept and this book represents that vision from the personal perspective of the author, whose background is in digital asset management. Accordingly, a central theme of this book relates to managing rich media files. However, many of the suggestions and recommendations in this book apply to a variety of digital content management disciplines, including text-based documents and Web content management and also touch on other key components of the media enterprise application suite. This book will refer to all the possible content that can be managed electronically as "digital content" and it will establish the term "digital content management" to describe the task of managing any digitally available content or information.

The motivation for this book was the fact that there is little opportunity today to learn about complex digital content management processes and practices in a product-neutral environment. Education in this field is mostly offered through product-driven education. Competitive pressure and a dramatic increase in digital content create the need for content management, and compliance laws generate another incentive to evaluate costly systems to control the flow of digital information. Despite these facts, there is a surprising lack of guidance and direction in this industry. There is an abundance of acronyms that describe nuances in product difference but very few standards or protocols.

The author's approach to large-scale content management is built on the fundamental belief that human experience should always be the center of innovation. Whereas most publications in this field concentrate solely on technology, features, and functionality, this book aims to incorporate the business processes and the view of the users, implementation teams, and stakeholders, who ultimately determine and drive the success of business ventures.

The goal for this book is to provide practical tips and expert advice on topics concerning planning, implementing, and improving larger interconnected content management systems and their components, as well as the processes surrounding these systems that need to be well understood and implemented simultaneously.

Who Should Read this Book

While technical in some areas, this book is not intended for engineers. This book is written for those readers who have some experience with managing digital content but wish to improve their understanding of content management. Readers rethinking the larger vision or expanding their existing system into new areas of the content lifecycle or the business process will find this book particularly useful. It is written for the people in charge of defining, planning, and implementing long term content management strategies and solutions.

Structure of this Book

This book consists of 11 chapters that can be read collectively or individually. Where appropriate, chapters include a clarification of terminology used in that chapter and each chapter ends with a summary of the covered issues. Dedicated chapters are devoted to those topics that are central to a successful long-term strategy for large-scale content management. The chapters vary from general concepts to very practical issues. Readers will also find various case studies that aim to bring clarity and descriptiveness to the issues raised in this book. The Resource section includes numerous links and resources so the reader can explore in-depth topics of particular interest.

Executive Summary

As consumer interactions with media shifts from traditional models to one-to-one relationships, media firms that achieve sophisticated control of content and robust tools to distribute and sell targeted content will succeed in capturing non-traditional media markets.

Organizations start to realize that digital content represents an increasingly important element of their business and this is true not only for media and entertainment companies. For many companies, the intellectual property (IP)—the core knowledge of an organization—is the most valuable asset. That IP is captured in digital files for various purposes: product manufacturing processes, instructions, training, research, brand equity, and more. Creating a comprehensive and all-inclusive roadmap for managing this value is becoming a strategic goal for many companies. Managing text-based content and rich media assets efficiently requires integrated content management systems and processes.

The digital content management industry is tremendously varied and continually evolving. While basic document repositories and image libraries are fairly standard nowadays, interconnected multi-functional systems are still developing. Consistency is needed for standards and practices, as well as for sound planning and realistic expectations for those companies seeking to implement solutions. The issues addressed in this book will hopefully save some organizations from costly missteps taken by others in the past.

The Digital Content Management Space

Chapter 4 defines the most commonly used technologies of digital content management (DCM), also known as digital asset management (DAM) that one must evaluate when considering a DCM system. One emerging concept in the industry is that of enterprise content management (ECM). ECM is still young, and there are varying opinions that fall under the ECM umbrella. The general agreement is that it is a complex and highly diversified industry. No vendor and integrator can claim expertise in all fields. However, the concept of the digital media enterprise goes much further than that of ECM. The larger business vision and the resulting strategies, processes, and practices are equally—if not more—important than technology. In addition, the strategies in terms of technology need to include a vision not only for the content management aspects but also for the interconnected data flows between content stores and business application such as subscription and transaction management, supply chain management, and more. This concept is explored in detail in Chapters 4, 6 and 9.

While the complexity and immaturity of the digital content space as a whole is a clear business risk, there are various organizations that have managed to produce significant return on investment (ROI) from initiatives in some segments of this space. The most prominent example is the pharmaceutical industry, which could no longer survive without sophisticated document management for regulatory approval. Some studios and broadcasters have proven impressive returns of DCM by cutting production times and time to market. There is broad consensus on one important element required for success with larger projects: Successful projects are driven by strategic senior management initiatives. Therefore, senior management education about digital content management, its risks, and its opportunities is an important step in any winning strategy.

What drives vision for the digital media enterprise is the realization that different vertical solutions, while successful in themselves, are not taking advantage of each other. More frequently than ever, content crosses the traditional dividing lines between operational units and media types. Martha Stewart Omnimedia is an example. Independent of the personal problems that affected the brand, Martha Stewart Omnimedia has been extremely successful with its clear vision of an interconnected content management strategy that shares assets across the vertical lines of print, video, Web, and retail. The future will belong to companies that can provide content to any consumer or business partner in the form and format requested in near real time. Additionally, those companies know who they deliver to, the demographics, the preferences and the "also likes."

As the costs for sophisticated content management systems are in the multi-million dollar range, it is very wise to begin the process with understanding the long-term trends of the market. By no means is this book suggesting building an all-encompassing large-scale, interconnected system today. In fact, the promise of ECM should be viewed with careful suspicion. But understanding the dynamics of the market is a valuable and important step toward preparing for the challenges to come and is a necessary basis for important decision in terms of technology platforms and system architecture.

These external elements will play a role in the solution to the content management problem, but they should not be the sole focus of the business case. As described in Chapters 1 and 6, equally important elements for defining a winning strategy are internal analysis and problem definition. Starting an expansion of exiting systems in well defined phases following a clear vision and defined strategy can support organization in overcoming vertical fragmentation and other limitations to the free flow of content and business data across the enterprise. That flow is the basis for flexibility and rapid development of new and targeted product offerings in new and traditional markets with known and new supply chains and delivery channels. Podcasting is just one example. Within days of launching the service, Apple had more than a million podcast subscribers. Forrester estimates podcast listeners could be growing to 12.3 million by 2010. Digital content management plays a key role in preparing media and entertainment companies for this future. Therefore it is the first building block of the digital media enterprise.

Trademarks

Adobe Creative Suite, Adobe Graphic Server

Microsoft Internet Explorer, Microsoft .net

Firefox

Plone

Zope®

IBM®

DB2® Content Manager

HP®

Java™

Mac World

Adobe Illustrator®

MS Visio®

QuarkXPress™

InDesign®

PowerPoint®

Flash®

Adobe®

Corbis®

Digimarc

ImageBridge™

MarcSpider™

Microsoft®

Ascent Media

Dreamweaver®

Firefox™

Safari™

Final Cut Pro®

Avid®

ENPS (Electronic News Production System for TV News)

QPS (Quark Publishing System for newspapers)

DuPont™

BEA Systems™

WebLogic Platform®

AquaLogic™

Cordys™

Cordys Business Collaboration Platform™

General Dynamics

IBM®

WebSphere® Platform

SAP®

SAP NetWeaver™

Sun Microsystems™

TIBCO® Software: BusinessWorks™

Sun's Java Virtual Machine (JVM™)

J2EE™

Enterprise Java Beans™

Windows®

Linux®

Synaptica®

Google™

Verity®

NAB Disclaimer

The opinions, findings, and conclusions expressed in this publication are those of the author(s) alone, and not necessarily those of the National Association of Broadcasters.

1 Defining the Starting Point and Direction of the Expansion

This chapter explores the need to define the various options and reasons to expand a digital content management across the enterprise and it will provide recommendation for the implementation planning of such an expansion.

Digital content management systems have been around for about 20 years. Document (or records) management systems have helped companies streamline text-based, content-related workflows and processes, such as government approval for products in the pharmaceutical industry. Web content management, the next evolution of managing content, has established itself as an important part of solving the growing challenge of managing the flow of information in digital form. Over the last few years, entertainment and publishing companies as well as many marketing organizations have come to look to digital asset management technologies and processes to streamline the production, review, approval, and distribution of rich media assets such as photos and videos.

This book will provide recommendations and case studies and will touch on three areas: text-based documents and records, Web site management, and rich media management. Chapter 3 will define document management (DM), digital content management (DCM), also known as Digital Asset Management (DAM), and Web content management (CM or WCM) in more detail.

One underlying assumption is that the reader's organization has experience with at least one existing digital content management project, potentially with a limited scope, that addresses a specific need such as an online library of stock photos/footage or learning objects, a marketing distribution portal, a collaborative work environment for the creation of content, or a system to manage the content published on the Web.

Phase Zero: Problem Definition

Defining the problem is the most important step toward solving it. Consider this anecdote about Albert Einstein, the ultimate authority on problem solving:

> *Einstein remarked that creativity is all about asking the right questions. When asked what he would do if given one hour to save the world, Einstein replied that he would spend 55 minutes to understand and formulate the problem, and 5 minutes to execute the solution. For complex business problems that require process changes and software development, it is vital that the right problems are identified in order to prevent costly design and implementation mistakes.*[1]

Defining the Current State

Before planning any extension of or addition to the system, one should allow for some examination of the system in use today. While some might know what the system can do, does everyone? The capabilities of the current system or process to manage content may not be apparent for stakeholders of other groups within the organization. It may be smart to involve one or more vendors or consultants in the expansion.

Even if the existing system will be replaced, important lessons can be learned from it. There are reasons why it is being replaced. It is highly recommended to capture those reasons as precisely as possible. One should note things such as:

- Business case overview including any return on investment (ROI) if available. What was the original business case? How has the system changed since then? How has the business changed?

- A description of the asset types managed in the system and the life cycle of the assets in the system. Different asset types might have different life cycles.

- A description of all user roles and use cases, including any administrators.

- The number of users per role.

- The number of assets by asset type in the system.

---

1. www.55minutes.com

- The frequency and quantity of new assets added to the system.

- Use of the system specific to geography, including time zones and languages.

Prior Lessons

The lessons learned by the organization during the implementation of the original system can be very valuable. This is true even if its initial implementation was a painful experience. However, too often, these lessons are not captured anywhere. Maybe nobody took notes or the primary planner for current expansion was not involved with the original implementation. In that case, contact members of the original implementation team and tap into their memories. Even if some team members are no longer working for the organization, they may be willing to share their experiences. Capturing the lessons learned from prior projects will save money, time, and nerves. Table 1.1 lists some questions to ask.

WHAT WORKED?	WHAT DID NOT WORK?
What did the implementation team do right in terms of planning, communication, and implementation?	What were the challenges in terms of planning, communication, and implementation?
What helped in setting correct expectations with stakeholders and users?	Were the initial expectations unrealistic? If so, how?
Did the vendor(s) provide any specific helpful support in terms of planning, communication, and implementation?	Did management misunderstand the objectives? If so, how?
What positive things did the users have to say about the process?	What were the vendor's challenges in terms of planning, communication, and implementation?
	What negative things do the users note about the current system?

TABLE 1.1 *Evaluating Past Implementations*

Capturing User Feedback

Getting detailed feedback about the existing system and about its implementation process is the first important step for scaling a system. Create a survey for the users to rate the current system. After this exercise, one should have vetted documents describing the system in comprehensive terms and describing the process of how the system was implemented. Not only will these documents help in the planning process, but they also represent a key element of the business case. Providing information about the current state and the lessons learned will build a solid foundation for recommendations with respect to future investments. Chapter 6, dedicated to building the business case, covers this in more detail.

Here is an inspiring article. "CMS Acceptance Testing" by Lisa Welchman provides good ideas for user testing but also user feedback in general. Welchman states "...it's important for users to understand before any code gets written exactly how they are going to work in the system and how it will impact their job."
The article can be found at www.cmswatch.com.

The result of proper planning should be a well-documented analysis of the current formal and informal processes and practices regarding creating, reviewing, approving, distributing, storing, reusing, and ultimately destroying content. From that analysis improved processes can be identified, and most likely technology can be used to improve efficiencies and control. With this background, the planning process can now move forward. The next step will be to define what kind of enhancements and expansions to the digital content management system are required.

Case Study

Zweites Deutsches Fernsehen (ZDF)

The following case study highlights the potential for cost savings and enhanced services. It discusses carefully examining current processes and technologies before changing or replacing them.

Background

ZDF, one of Europe's largest public broadcasters, had a legacy system called Fernseh Data Base (FDB) that was supporting thousands of concurrent users on a terminal server based system. The FDB system was not capable of supporting integration with production and newsroom systems, nor was it able to provide video browsing functionality.

CONTINUED ▶

CONTINUED ▶

Solution

ZDF approached Blue Order, a German digital content management company, to provide a new solution that would leave FDB in place for many of the users, but would provide additional functionality for up to 800 "super-users" with integration across production and newsroom platforms.

Result

It was not necessary to incur the expense of totally replacing a solution that still met the needs of the majority of users. ZDF also benefited from the streamlined workflows that could be achieved with the integration available with Blue Order's solution.

   This case study was first published at the Henry Stewart Digital Asset Management Symposium in New York, on May 10, 2005, by Jeremy Bancroft, former sales and marketing director, EMEA, Blue Order Ltd. It is published here with the permission of Blue Order

   Contact: Christina Seemann, Manager Marketing Services, Blue Order AG.

Defining the Expansion

As with all complex systems, it is important to ensure that the meaning of "expansion" is clear. It can mean different things to different people. There are many possible reasons for expanding a system—too many to list. This section defines three ways a system can grow and should help clarify and communicate goals for the expansion. A company might need to expand in more than one way. If at all possible, plan the expansion in phases and implement one at a time.

Scale in Size

In the traditional sense of scaling an application, a significant number of new users and/or content are added to the system. If all new users are able to use the system in the same language (no multi-lingual interfaces) and if all new content can be categorized by the existing taxonomy, this is most likely only a hardware issue. These issues are addressed in Chapter 8, which deals with scaling the hardware and software. However, it may be necessary to consider the added work for the administrator in supporting and managing user accounts. Quite often, a company will need to rethink the system taxonomy or data structure if multiplying the

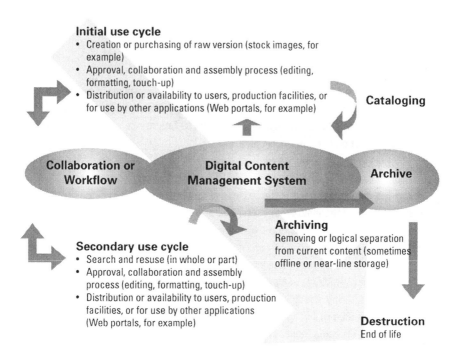

Initial use cycle
- Creation or purchasing of raw version (stock images, for example)
- Approval, collaboration and assembly process (editing, formatting, touch-up)
- Distribution or availability to users, production facilities, or for use by other applications (Web portals, for example)

Cataloging

Collaboration or Workflow

Digital Content Management System

Archive

Secondary use cycle
- Search and resuse (in whole or part)
- Approval, collaboration and assembly process (editing, formatting, touch-up)
- Distribution or availability to users, production facilities, or for use by other applications (Web portals, for example)

Archiving
Removing or logical separation from current content (sometimes offline or near-line storage)

Destruction
End of life

FIGURE 1.1 *The Content Life Cycle*

number of assets by a factor of 10 or more. Chapters 10 and 11 are focused on expanding the taxonomy and data structure.

Expand Vertically

A vertical expansion adds an additional aspect of the life cycle of the existing assets within the system. The life cycle of an asset can usually be defined in the same manner, as shown in Figure 1.1. This applies regardless of whether the company is a media company whose digital assets represent its core business, or whether the organization is using a digital content management system to manage marketing materials or a specific element of a value chain such as product labels.

Most likely, there will be additional formal and informal approval processes between the steps of the life cycle, often driven by complex dependencies and rules. The existing system likely addresses or at least supports some of these processes in the organization for certain assets today.

For example, an organization might currently manage the distribution of marketing material to the distribution channel or to the direct sales force, or both.

One example of a vertical expansion would be the inclusion of the creation process by ingesting material prior to final approval, using the system for an online approval process. The process would ensure brand compliance, legal compliance, and such. Approved assets might then automatically move into the existing structure for management and distribution.

Expand Horizontally

The author defines a horizontal expansion as adding entirely new areas of business to the system. For example, a company might distribute marketing material to a certain channel, but now it wants to manage internal email archiving for compliance reasons. Or the company is a publishing house and, while one division has made good use of the system, managers wish to introduce it to a new division that has a different asset life cycle (workflow). For example, a printing division likely has a different workflow for assets than does a TV division.

Recommendations for the Implementation Planning

As the earlier case studies, the business case and technical requirements of digital content management system implementations are not the same, even in the same industry sector. However, there are a few universal truths about implementing large scale, potentially disruptive, technologies that should be highlighted. Additionally there are a few specifically digital content-related issues that might be well worth the attention when building an implementation plan.

Phased Approach

There have been many articles and a few books written about the advantages of breaking complex projects into smaller logical steps. However, it cannot be stressed enough that the most-violated rule of sound project management is aiming for the "Big Bang." This approach tries to address various possible business problems at once and aims to present the solution for all of them together.

> This book and this article provide more in-depth information about phased project management: "How to Run Successful Projects III: The Silver Bullet (3rd Edition)" by Fergus O'Connell (Pearson Professional Education) and "Don't Boil the Ocean" by Rob Zimmelman, a well written article, can be found at: www.rockwoodgroup.com.

Naturally, vendors and integrators alike have a tendency to expand the project for monetary gain. Therefore, it falls to the internal implementation team and the internal stakeholders to ensure sound planning. However, few companies have staff skilled in enterprise-level technical deployments; in fact, it is often the internal stakeholders who drive the project scope beyond the comfort level of the team ultimately assigned to manage the implementation.

The senior management team will have to step in here and provide strong leadership, allowing for guidance in sound planning and phased implementation. As will be mentioned repeatedly in this book, adjusting the internal structures or governance to enable an organization to manage a larger digital content management strategy will require senior management to be involved. Expanding a content management system across the enterprise should become a strategic company initiative.

This book tries to highlight areas where a complex implementation can and should be broken into small chunks. Specifically, the first few phases should include very distinct project goals that are well defined and ideally carry limited risk and complexity. An example could be a simple archive of images or stock footage, a PowerPoint library, or an archive of text documents. As each type of content brings its own processes and challenges, it usually will make sense to break the phases down along the lines of content types. The same can be said about the user groups. While the number of users is not so much the issue, it is the functions or roles the users play that matters. Each role might have distinctive needs and expectations on how content is searched, presented, and delivered. Therefore, it can make good sense to limit not only the initial number of file types but also the number of different roles that access them.

It should be made clear that the overall vision and planning should always be for the longer term. Scalability, flexibility, and integration options are very important. At the same time, the flexibility of enterprise-scale applications can become initially also a project risk, as it will take some experience to define which of the potentially many options is right, provided the assumption that there is one right way. So, solving minor business problems first will not only allow the building of a progression of little successes, but it will also train the users, administrators, and implementation team on how to implement the solutions. As the team and organization matures, the problems can become more complex, and multiple business problems might be addressed in one phase.

Maturity is not only needed in terms of technology and understating of the chosen software applications, it is also needed in terms of business models and financial calculations. If budgets and returns are not meeting the expectations, adjustments need to be made and the business case might change significantly. If initial project phases are trying to accomplish too much, it will become very complex to pinpoint overruns and miscalculations. Most organizations will have had little experience in measuring return on investment of large-scale digital content management, so mistakes are unavoidable. One goal should be to keep these mistakes small by limiting the scope of the initial phases.

Lastly, limited scope is essential from a change management perspective. Proof to the users that the changes which will be introduced are not entirely disrupting their work environment and that the new features, tools and processes are really helping them do a better job is critical to the success of a new system. Naturally, not everyone will be happy, but as the trust in the new tools grows, the organization will be ready to take on more challenging and larger projects.

Project Management

This book will not try to explain sound project management practices, as many books exist on that topic. However, certain digital content-specific schedule mistakes are common. Chapter 10 and 11 detail the topics of taxonomy and metadata models. In many content management projects—digital and otherwise—it is the data model and classification system that will become one of the key factors for success. Building these data models for larger interconnected systems is very complex and will be a moving target as with new functionalities new options will appear. There is no formula by which the required time can be estimated, but defining the data that is used in existing workflows, libraries, and distribution systems takes time. Then this data has to be mapped into the new tools, archives, and systems. User feedback for the initial models is absolutely necessary and changes to the proposed models are guaranteed.

While many projects do not plan enough time for the development of taxonomies and data models, other projects do the opposite. The most successful approach is probably some middle ground where thorough research is not holding up a phased implementation with initially limited scope to allow early and constant validation and competency build up.

If one rule can be set it might be that the time and resources required to define and implement taxonomies and data models will never be less that that required for the technical and functional specification of any solution.

Another aspect easily overlooked in an often technology-focused project planning approach is that of organizational readiness and governance. This issue is discussed in Chapter 2. Here it should be stressed that it will take effort and time to define who will manage new tools and processes and refine practices. New skill sets might be required and resources need training not only on technology but on processes and practices. More experienced staff may be recruited but even that takes time. There is a limited supply of experienced content management managers and administrators. Finding these resources who might also need to have background in a specific vertical can take a long time. The aspects of governance and change management are intertwined. For many organizations multiple long management and off site meetings will be required to ensure everybody is on the same page.

Strategy Corrections

A third aspect that impacts the project plan is that of iterative versus linear planning. In general, project plans are visualized as a linear time line. That makes sense because time is linear. However, large scale innovation is everything but linear. It is iterative. As each project phase is implemented, it will result in new knowledge, new options, and changed expectations. Everything discussed above will impact the project plan in a continuous flow of user feedback, budget, and milestone adjustments and so on. It is therefore very important to set the expectation that a key deliverable of every phase is a new and adjusted project plan or project charter for the next phase or phases.

This iterative approach is unfortunately not often taught in project management 101 classes. The business vision is what counts, not how we get there. The strategy has to be flexible. If the ultimate goal is to build a new revenue stream, for example, than anything that will accomplish that goal is what is important. It is not important to stick to a specific project plan that was created with limited knowledge and experience of the technologies and processes involved.

Of course, in the business reality, there are certain milestones that need to be met. Dependencies among different projects and other key elements might force a certain linear approach. However, iterative planning is not necessarily opposed to the idea of meeting milestones; it is just another step of a phased approach. Managing the balance between changing approaches and a predictable project plan is another element of required maturity with will grow over time.

Summary

This chapter discussed concrete planning steps that are often overlooked: defining the problem and the expansion. As the case studies highlighted, it is very helpful to understand all current processes and systems that manage content before replacing them, and it is useful to define what kind of expansion in digital content management abilities the organization is striving for. Any minute and every penny cut from the initial business analysis and problem definition is paid in hours and dollars later. Solution definition for content management projects is primarily a business process definition and reengineering challenge and to a lesser degree driven by technology decisions.

2 Preparing the Organization for the Expansion

This chapter dives into important concepts that any organization considering a larger digital content management project should embrace: the limits of technology, as well as the need for change management, governance models, and evolving competencies.

These issues are not typically discussed in detail at conferences or in publications, as this industry tends to focus on technology alone. Therefore, these issues deserve examination in detail.

Technology Alone Will Not Solve the Problem

While technology is an important part of any digital content management solution, it is the processes and practices that really make the difference. Take the introduction of the telephone as an example. If a company had a problem with selling its products or services, a telephone could provide a new and efficient means for the sales team to reach target clients at lower cost. However, if the sales team does not know how to pitch its value preposition, a telephone won't help much.

In the same sense, it can be argued that if an organization is unable to manage a digital file system, it most likely will be unable to manage a complex content management system. In order to represent content to users more intuitively and with increased control, many new processes but also many old processes need to be defined, refined, implemented, enforced, managed, advertised, explained, and so on. In many cases, this is entirely independent of technology.

> Many projects fail to define the real problems underlying the companies' needs for content management. In some cases, "new technology" replaces systems that would work just fine if used properly, and if the processes surrounding these tools were well thought through.

This technology-focused approach to problem solving is not surprising when taking into consideration the significant effort by the product marketing teams to send one clear message: "There is a product out there that can do this" (whatever "this" might be). Even if a product fails, the voices saying that it was "just the wrong product" are well-tuned and difficult to ignore. Very few companies selling the product that does "this" encourage organizations to think and not spend their money. If the focus is on technology decisions before the problem is truly understood, there is a danger of quickly becoming distracted and engulfed by the marketing "circus".

Valuable time and resources may be tied up in evaluating products, preventing the organization from focusing on defining the real issues. This has happened over and over again in the content management industry. Technology is sexy and promises fast results. Research, whiteboards, and interviews are boring, but those tasks are the most important element of planning a larger content management system.

Referring back to the telephone example: Inside sales departments today do not spend much thought on phones. Although phone systems can become very complex and costly, it is the scripts, incentives, territories, and campaign management that make or break an inside sales team. The same is mostly true for digital content management, where the processes are more important than the tools. And, if introducing new tools, the required changes in the processes should be considered carefully.

Change Management

Another big issue that most companies underestimate when considering even smaller content management systems is that of change management. Any new technology or application has an impact on the people who use it. Change never comes easily. It cannot be stressed enough that managing the impact of the change is the one of the most underestimated tasks in implementing or expanding systems, large and small.

Following are a few tips and examples of how to avoid that pain and how to manage change by involving the user community in the planning, implementation, and improvement or expansion of the system.

User Involvement

Administrators, end users, as well as management stakeholders, should be involved in the very first planning steps. All stakeholders must be regularly involved in the implementation process. Users who will be affected by the upcoming changes in their work environment should understand the vision and strategy for that change. While this may seem obvious and of paramount importance, it is often overlooked by implementation teams.

> The most important concept to stress to users or teams when managing change should be that the system is not built for the content, but for the people who use that content. Essentially, it is not a content management system; rather, it is a user-managed content system.

One effective way to manage the system expansion is to break it down into logical blocks of use cases that are simple enough to be described in a single meeting. (More on this suggestion in Chapter 4). The affected users should be part of the planning meetings for these use cases. Members of the user group who are also members of the implementation team do not count, as it is important for others to provide feedback to them. One should not proof one's own work.

A good example is the metadata for a given use case or file type. At the start of almost every project, it is common that specification documents include very long lists of file descriptors and file attributes that are all somewhat related to the use case or file type. But in just as many cases, the users will only use three or four attributes to search and identify a file. Without feedback from the users, it is not possible to define which attributes are necessary and will be used. If users are part of the decision about which attributes to make available on a search page, chances are significantly increased that the search page they help create will be useful and that it will be used as intended.

In addition, content has both formal and informal routes through any organization today. Hopefully, the official route is known, but it is necessary to hear from hands-on users about how they deal with the exceptions and breakdowns of the process. Other users might never have known what happens to Joe's tasks when Joe is sick, but now it becomes crucial in defining the correct system setup.

Finally, keep in mind that people in the organization have some level of pride in what they do. This pride is proportional to the motivation of any team. If the users are allowed to influence the new tools and processes, they will more likely take pride in these new elements of their jobs. When their motivation is higher, their willingness to change is increased dramatically. They will have a sense of ownership of the change; it is theirs, just as much as the company's.

Organizational Change

It is important to remember that end users will not be the only ones affected by changes. The change process must start long before the system is completed. It starts the moment the idea of content management is presented to the potential stakeholders on the management team. Every stakeholder in the process will be affected in some way. The IT team will need to evaluate and eventually embrace some new technology that might or might not fit exactly into their "dream environment." The CFO or controller might have to accept new expenditures and different revenue models than they are used to. Mid-level managers will have to allow users to join planning meetings and, perhaps, plan for new positions and identify new skill sets they know nothing about. The person planning the expansion, no matter what their role is today, will have to deal with all of this in some form. This leads to the next topic of this chapter: Governance and Competency.

Case Study

Harcourt, Inc.

Background

Harcourt, Inc., a member of the Reed Elsevier Group plc, is a publisher in the educational and trade sector. The business challenge was to ensure the effective governance of digital asset management initiatives at the Harcourt businesses, without forcing the use of one technology platform or process as the business units have very different needs. For Harcourt, managed content represents part of the core value of the company. CONTINUED ▶

CONTINUED ▶

Solution

Harcourt established a corporate shared services group to oversee the analysis, selection, and implementation of DAM solutions. The service group determined a base set of standards for technology to meet, a core set of metadata that each business unit should use in their DAM system, and staffing requirements within business units for the management of DAM. Within this group, the role of Director of Digital Asset Management is a company-wide resource that can advise, facilitate and champion digital asset management efforts. The role can support needs analysis, technology acquisition and implementation. The role is also a resource for process and practices such as developing standards.

   For business unit staffing, the corporate group has established the role of Intellectual Property Resource (IPR) or Digital Asset Manager with librarians as direct reports. The business unit IPR/DAM staff manages the metadata, user set up, and training administrative tasks for the DAM systems, and manages collection development. They work closely with departments within the business unit, but also collaborate with each other on best practices across business units.

Result

Harcourt, through various successes and challenges, has built its competency in regard to digital asset management. Through digital asset management staffing at the corporate and business unit levels, accumulated knowledge is available to the various Harcourt businesses and senior management. As the digital asset management industry matures, Harcourt is well positioned to leverage technology and best practices.

   Published with the permission of Harcourt, Inc.

Governance Models and Evolving Competencies

The content management project will hopefully result in new and improved processes and use of efficiency enhancing technologies. An organization might introduce new service offerings to internal and/or external clients. In the best case the organization's overall content and, with that, its valuable intellectual property, is now more secure and at the same time more available to the people who need it. However, the new processes and tools need to be managed beyond the point of implementation.

Governance models define the new management tasks and the roles required for managing, refining, and continuously educating the organization about the new processes, services, and technologies. Embedding the new governance structure into the existing management functions is also part of the change process. Industry insiders have a saying: content management is a profession, not solely a technology. The competency of this profession needs to become part of the organization on various levels, from taxonomy specialists/librarians to departmental leads, all the way up to the potential VP of IP or Chief Knowledge Officer (CKO). As with any other structure, the right governance model depends on many factors and varies from organization to organization.

Despite the many different potential governance models, there is one common thread: most companies are entirely ignorant of the fact that new governance models and education are needed on an ongoing basis. For smaller point solutions the responsibilities are often loaded onto existing employees who might or might not be prepared for this task. In many cases the IT team finds itself suddenly in charge of complex workflows and intellectual property whose business use cases are entirely foreign to the workings of an IT team. While for smaller systems this "sink or swim" approach to governance sometimes works, it will be futile if practiced in larger deployments.

The digital content management industry is often called immature. That might exclude the most basic document repository or image library, but for interconnected, multi-functional systems it is mostly true. Maturity is needed in the form of standards and practices, but it is also needed in terms of sound planning and realistic expectations on the side of the companies seeking to implement solutions.

Case Study

Rafael Ltd.

Background

Rafael Ltd. in Israel is a 5,000-person R&D company focused on defense technologies and systems. Rafael is comprised of four business units, an IT department, and a thin corporate. Since knowledge is the main asset in Rafael, a Chief Knowledge Officer (CKO) was appointed, and a very wide knowledge management (KM) initiative began taking place at the end of 2001. Some of the most important solutions are a number of content management (CM) systems that were developed as part of this initiative: CONTINUED ▶

CONTINUED ▶

- A patent pending 'light Enterprise Content Management (ECM)' ("MATRIX") based on the concept of Network centric CM
- Another Content Management System (CMS) ("SUNSHINE") based on the above content, which currently serves Sales and Marketing people.
- A CMS ("NYMPH") that gives a comprehensive solution to the management of Know-How (delivering procedures, standards, lessons learnt, tips, templates, etc… in the context it is needed)
- A CMS which helps in conducting and retrieving AARs and Lessons learnt
- A CMS for information regarding professional conferences.
- A simple CMS for the organization's procedures.
- In addition, there are about 200 collaborative sites, which also include content.

One major question was: who is in charge for what? Who is in charge for the definition of the solutions? Who is in charge of the development? Who is in charge of the adoption? Who is in charge of the content?

To make things even more complicated, there are a number of interested parties involved:

- The IT department
- The CKO and his staff (4)
- Technical point of contacts (Each business unit has technical points of contact that take part in the planning and the adoption of information systems)
- Content experts
- The audiences.

Solution

The solution is based on the following principles, applied in all the above cases:

- The IT department provides the best tools, integrating with existing information systems, and setting the standards for the limits of flexibility given to the users.
- The KM team provides methodology, advice, and in some cases, concrete help in the organization of the content
- The point of contacts are the support team in the business units, applying the standards and methodology, and physically helping in building the sites
- The content experts are responsible for the constant update of the content.
- The lines between all the above are very gray, and good personal relationships and trust is needed for the whole system to work.

One other aspect that is important to mention is the number of content experts in each of the systems mentioned above:

- In most collaborative intranet sites, there are 1-8 people that contribute content on a regular basis (not including the Q&A section) CONTINUED ▶

CONTINUED ▶

- In the CMS serving the sales and marketing, hundreds of people contribute content, and the governance of that system is a separate case study on its own.
- Similarly, every worker can add content to the "professional conferences CMS" – since each person is best qualified to describe the conference that he (or she) took part in.
- In the Know-how systems (NYMPH, the procedures system, and the lessons learnt system) only chosen content experts can add content, since the content represents the company know-how and must be accurate

Result

While the process of building awareness and competency around the greater content management challenge continues, the company has implemented a number of content management systems, one of which is a patent pending 'light ECM', and established a system where different parts of the organization support each other, and using the synergy created to improve the chance that the above CMSs will yield business benefits for the company

Published with the permission of Rafael Ltd.

Contact: Yair Dembinsky, CKO, Rafael Ltd., dambi10@zahav.net.il

Summary

The points made in this chapter are intended to highlight the most costly mistakes:

When a solution approach has been defined, involving the users and careful management of the change process are key ingredients for reaching the envisioned ROI.

The larger the strategy, the deeper the change also to the management structure. Defining the right governance model for the approach is imperative for long-term success.

Due to the complexity of large-scale content management and the need for refined governance and change processes, it is not easy to find highly skilled and unbiased advice for both technical and human aspects. The marketing slant to most product education and trade shows, as well as the leading analysts' "Magic Quadrants," oversimplify the view to a degree that makes them almost useless. Technology vendors and integrators rarely make good change managers. Their focus is usually on the technology and not on the people who use or implement it. Use the resources below to find truly unbiased support. That independent voice should help in the planning stage by providing industry expertise and inside knowledge, as well as help with change management and the definition of governance models.

3 Definition of Technologies and Products

Anyone who has been around the field of digital content management for some time might have read the attempts from various writers to define and clarify the difference between those solutions described by the innumerable acronyms of the industry at large. Unfortunately, significant confusion still exists. This chapter will contrast digital asset management (DAM) systems, document management (DM) and records management (RM) systems, and Web content management systems (WCM or WCMS) and enterprise content management (ECM) systems. Along the way, one may learn what kind of system or combination of systems is right for one's expanding strategy.

A High Level Overview of Digital Content Management Systems

To begin with, one should remember that most acronyms and abbreviations are creations of marketing minds and more often than not they were used to build a new "category" independent of any potentially closely related category. This was done so each marketing department could claim it is "The world leader in [...]". Following some success in that marketing strategy, other vendors picked up the terms because they saw a marketing advantage in doing so.

As a result, one larger category like digital asset management (DAM) can have many subcategories like media asset management (MAM), brand resource management (BRM), marketing content management (MCM), and many more that are too close to clearly differentiate in this chapter. Products that claim a stake in one or some of these acronym-rich market segments are by no means identical in feature sets and functionality and do not adhere to any standard. In fact, one DAM system can be quite different from the next, and the same is true for any of the other market segments.

At the same time, it does make sense to articulate and group systems in some form of category because the field of digital content management is a very broad industry with fuzzy edges, and some overlap into other established fields like customer relationship management (CRM), enterprise resource management (ERM, and other business intelligence (BI) and e-commerce systems. It can be very helpful to match the initial business need to one segment that follows true logical lines and not just marketing trends. This can help to focus research and makes the number of applicable articles, books and the trade shows manageable.

> More specialized categories exist but are not defined in this chapter. A few more common categories that might deserve attention when expanding digital content management strategy are listed here and in the resource section:
> * Knowledge Management (KM)
> * Digital Rights Management (DRM), explained further in Chapter 5
> * Learning Content Management Systems (LCMS)
> * Marketing Content Management or Marketing Automation (subset of DAM)•
>   E-mail Management (Provided by many DM vendors)

Definition of DM, DAM, CM, and ECM

The heart of most digital content management systems is a set of core functionalities, some of which might be part of a vendor's proprietary code, while other functionalities might be delivered through third-party tools. The four core elements (or "engines") are also described as the digital content management back end:

1. The content or asset management engine: This is the core of every system, and it builds a searchable representation of the repository utilizing a relational database in most cases. The core logic will handle transactions such as check-in/checkout, upload, and download.

2. The metadata and relationship index: This includes descriptors, administrative data, and versions, and in addition to other hierarchical, peer to peer,

parent/child or lineage relationships.

3.   The search engine: It can perform searches against the above defined index and relationships, and also searches other external data from a text indexing tool or the public internet, for example.

4.   The security logic: It defines the privileges and permissions that determine who can see and do what with which objects.

There are two associated back end tools required to drive a complete solution. They are described as:

1.   The workflow or collaboration engine: Schedules and defines tasks in serial or parallel progression. Tasks may also be rule based (allowing 'if …then…' logic). Basic rule-based workflow is part of many solutions. Large-scale workflow engines are available as standalone plug-in engines at a wide range of cost and flexibility. Just google "workflow engine" for a list of options.

2.   The business transaction engine: Tracks transactions that are not necessarily part of the core content management system, but that are important for the business owner—order acceptance, order fulfillment, and basic e-commerce—that are managed and tracked for reporting and analysis or data mining.

To be taken seriously in this market, a product will include at least some combination of these elements and might or might not be capable of extending or integrating with the other aspects. Many point solutions, which might be all a company needs initially, may not need the full back end suite. For example, a simple image library or video archive may need only the core elements.

What decides the segment that a product or solution will fall into are the peripheral tools and systems built around these back end elements. There is more overlap between products than the tables and explanations below might suggest. The goal of this section is to provide some clarity of the differences and core functionalities. The second half of this chapter explores how these categories apply to the reality of an expanding system.

Document Management (DM)

According to Tony Byrne of CMS Watch, "Document management products function to help companies better manage the creation and flow of [mostly text-based] documents through the help of databases and workflow engines that encapsulate metadata and business rules."[1]

---

1. www.cmswatch.com/Features/OpinionWatch/FeaturedOpinion/?feature_id-53

Table 3.1 and Figure 3.1 define some of the specific tools and processes that distinguish DM from other categories, as well as some examples of the file types typically managed with a DM solution and some examples for the business case of a DM system.

TOOLS AND PROCESSES/ (build on the back end)	DM FILE TYPES	BUSINESS USE
Capture or scan-and-capture text content in full or by zones with optical character recognition (OCR)	Everything text based	Collaboration and management of the following:
Integration with text processing tools such as MS Word, Adobe Acrobat, and others for ingest of other documents.	Paper	Contracts
	File output from word processing and spreadsheets such as MS Word or MS Excel	Documentation/ Manuals
Allow the definition of content components within a document.		Policy and Procedures
Assemble documents or document segments for reuse.	PDF	Forms
Manipulate documents, e.g., remove or rearrange documents or elements as well as redact text for some readers.	Text output or print stream from a computing system such as financial statements (e.g. COLD)	Research
		Applications for regulatory product approval
Allow storing of text effectively, often in a variety of different formats, including native formats and XML.		Statements
Provide text-specific search features such as fuzzy logic, proximity and natural language search as well as multiple language capabilities.	In more advanced systems you will have the option to load XML documents and fragments.	Articles
		Reports
		Correspondence
Apply metadata at varying levels within the document.		Case files
Present meaningful search results leveraging metadata and text summaries.	Other images and multimedia files, as generic binaries.	General office documents
Records Management will also include some storage and tracking technology that ensures the controlled retention of the content including special storage technology such as Write Once Read Many (WORM) devices.	and more...	and more...
Limited usage tracking.		
and more...		

TABLE 3.1 *Definition of Specific Tools and Processes for DM*

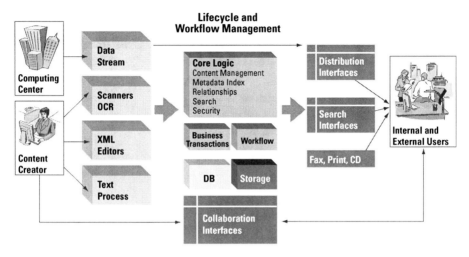

FIGURE 3.1 *Simplified DM Logical Flow*

Digital Asset Management (DAM)

DAM deals with rich media that often has a visual aspect more important than the textual content. The Table 3.2 and Figure 3.2 describe tools and process for DAM.

TOOLS AND PROCESSES (build on the back end)	DAM FILE TYPES	BUSINESS USE
Image manipulation/transformation for stored proxies and on the fly requests like resizing or color conversion.	Visually Rich Files	Collaboration and Management of:
	Images	Multimedia Press Kits
Video indexing of speech to text, speaker ID, Face ID, closed captioning and more.	Logos and Line Art	
	Designed Documents like QuarkXPress, Adobe InDesign and Illustrator	Multimedia Sales Kits
Video transcoding for proxies and on the fly request for lower resolution or different encoding (MPEG vs. Real vs. QuickTime vs. Media Player)		Multimedia General Marketing
Rendering of Web-ready visual representations of content	Audio	Multimedia Training Material
	Video	
Parsing of embedded data such as IPTC/XMP and others	Animation like Flash	Video on Demand (VOD)
Text indexing (overlap with DM and CM)	CAD	

TOOLS AND PROCESSES (build on the back end)/	DAM FILE TYPES	BUSINESS USE
Image recognition tools for visual searches (find images like this)	3-D HTML PowerPoint and more…	Rich Media Libraries like: Image Libraries Video Libraries Font Libraries (incl. style sheets) Logo Libraries PowerPoint Libraries and more…
Tools and plug-ins for the native or creative applications (authoring tools) to allow seamless access to the repository (QuarkXPress, Adobe suite of desktop and server applications, video tools like Final Cut Pro, Virage, Telestream, and also CAD, Flash and 3-D applications)		
Seamless linking and access to compound documents (Master template and linked files)		
Tools to handle very large files (multiple GB in video production for example)		
Present visually rich content and search results in the most meaningful and flexible way to users		
Watermarking of still and moving images		
Assemble assets for reuse (video play lists, image sets, PowerPoint presentations)		
and more…		

TABLE 3.2 *Tools and processes for DAM*

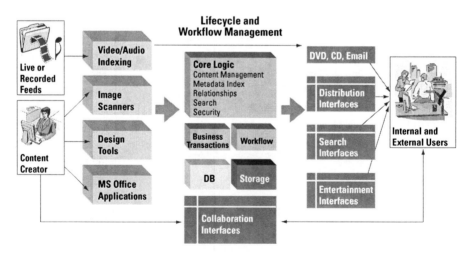

FIGURE 3.2 *Simplified DAM Logical Flow*

Content Management (CM)

Content management is: *"A software solution used to create, maintain and control a Web site."*[2] CM solutions are different from DAM and DM in that the latter are primarily repositories that allow varying degrees of collaboration in the creation and distribution process. The final products of DAM and DM can be distributed in many ways; print, CD/DVD, Web, fax, television, and more. CM solutions are focused on publication via the Web. Version control and searchable repositories are less important. Ensuring that the currently published (viewable) information is correct and easily editable by the right content creator is the most important element.

TOOLS AND PROCESSES (build on the back end)/	CM FILE TYPES	BUSINESS USE
Flexible publishing and authoring templates for static and dynamic pages	Any file that can represent information on a Web site	Collaboration and Management of the following:
Text indexing and search options	HTML in all flavors like DHTML	Portals
Tools and plug-ins to authoring tools like text processing programs, Dreamweaver or XML editors	XML	Web sites
Organization of Web site navigation and links	Graphics	Intranets
Input tools for online forms and user feedback	PDF documents	Extranets
Allow defining segments of the smallest reusable part of any content.	Lower resolution streaming video	E-commerce
Financial transaction tools	Streaming Audio	Web-Based Customer Service and Support
and more…	and more…	and more…

TABLE 3.3 *Tools and Processes for CM*

The unfortunate reality is that the peripheral tools described in the first column of the tables above are not necessarily built or integrated in a clean separation from the core logic that drives the product or solution. In most cases, a mish-mash of proprietary code keeps everything working together. Even if it is common to use the same tools for the same tasks (such as Adobe Graphic Server (AGS) for image manipulation or hierarchical storage management (HSM) technology to manage storage and archiving), the implementation will vary from vendor to vendor.

---

2. www.komodocms.com

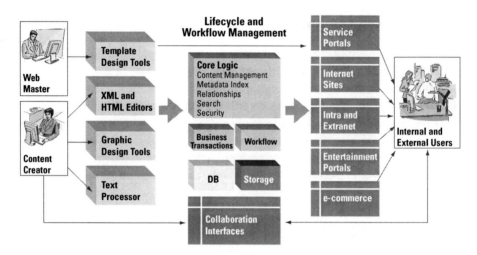

FIGURE 3.3 *Simplified CM Logical Flow*

After having defined the three categories, note now that defining categories becomes less useful as the system expands to include various classes of content and interconnect their workflows. At that stage the question is how to build a system that solves various issues around digital content and the interconnected but different life cycles of that content.Most likely the result is a morphed system that does not really fit any of the traditional definitions.

Enterprise Content Management (ECM)

James Robertson of Step Two Designs summarized that an enterprise content management system "consists of a core Web content management system, with additional capabilities to manage a broader range of organizational information. This often consists of document management, records management, digital asset management or collaboration features."[3]

ECM is now often used to describe any combination of digital content management systems developed to solve any number of management and collaboration tasks for an organization. That makes the use of ECM so broad that it is almost useless other than to define something really big and complicated.

One cannot find ECM systems that deliver all in one out of the box. Only in the past two years have DAM, DM, and CM systems been identified as the combined

---

3. www.steptwo.com.au/papers/cmb_definition/

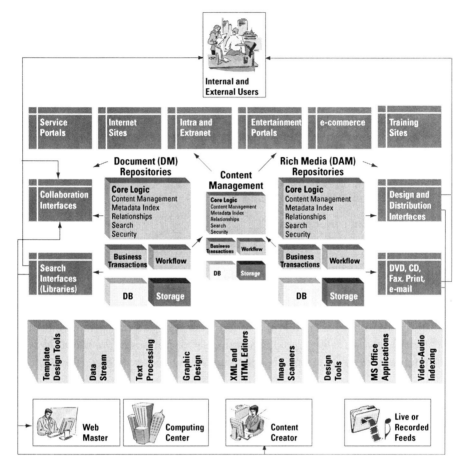

FIGURE 3.4 *Simplified ECM Logical Flow*

core to any unified content strategy. Users of many larger interconnected systems must duplicate the core functionalities to get the peripherals needed. Vendors in the ECM space have the same problem. For example, when the CM company bought the DAM vendor, they most likely ended up with two totally different approaches and potentially very different technologies they now need to integrate into their "Unified Technology Platform".

Building Your Own ECM

The good news is that vendors are starting to recognize the need for more modular products to reach a broader acceptance with integrators and larger service providers. It has become fashionable in this industry to speak about "open architecture," "open standards," and also services oriented architecture (SOA). A sample question could be: Can the company or its preferred integrator swap the text or video indexing tool with a tool of the company's choice or can only the vendor make such a change? These issues are discussed further in Chapters 8 and 9.

A larger integrated system will most likely have requirements that stretch across at least the DAM, CM, and DM set of tools and solutions described above. When defining requirements for a larger integrated system, the three guiding principles are:

1. True extensibility open architecture, available application programming interfaces APIs and separation of elements)

2. Scalability and performance

3. Functionality

Functionality in this case is defined in relationship to the business needs and the life cycle of the content to be managed. The goal is to build open systems that solve business problems now and in the future. There is no reason to align systems with the bells and whistles that the vendors are trying to sell at the moment. It might make sense to select a product that has fewer features or pre-packaged solutions, but is more easily extensible due to better and deeper defined APIs.

Large interconnected systems will require significant services to be designed, built, tested, and implemented. For most vendors in the digital content management space, "services" are their fastest growing revenue source. As these systems are implemented, they will immediately bring up new requirements and change requests not only because business needs change, but also because the new system in itself will introduce new opportunities and processes changes. The constant need to change and adapt is one of the main reasons flexibility is more important that completeness of features (other than those to address in the short term).

Interesting and encouraging developments in the open source community promise new open systems particularly for Web content management with much cleaner separation of core functionality and peripheral features. Plone (built on Zope) is currently the most complete solution. For a list of additional open source systems, see the OS CMS Directory. Some vendors, like ClearStory Systems with its Enterprise Media Server (EMS), IBM with Content Manager, and HP with the Digital Media Platform (DMP), have built platforms that are intended to be cleanly separated engines. Both open source and proprietary systems have been used in the field by CONTINUED ►

CONTINUED ▶   vendor-independent staff to successfully build entire solutions. The adoption of the first content management-focused Java standard, JSR170, is another encouraging sign. For additional information, see the Resources section.

However, development on this level will require highly skilled developers and more involved project planning with very well-defined requirements documents. Therefore, these industry developments might or might not help in the current situation. Everyone who is interested in building integrated large-scale solutions should encourage these developments and express a clear desire for more open systems toward proprietary vendors, small and large.

Summary

Large interconnected DCM systems are best viewed not as software products but as a system of different interconnected technologies and refined business processes. The planning, implementation, and maintenance of these systems will require specific knowledge and skills that organizations can build over time with help from independent service providers and consultants.

In conclusion, here is one final recommendation. While this chapter focuses on the technical aspects of the larger content management strategy, there is a big human factor in any large system implementation, as discussed in Chapter 2. Typically, most efficiency and productivity loss stems from failed change management and not necessarily from failed technology. If the users of the systems are not embracing the new tools and processes, it is unlikely that they will.

4 System Definition Recommendations and Advanced Concepts

While the first chapters introduced more general issues about building larger digital content management systems, this chapter focuses on specific issues and provides actionable advice for the future system definition. For information on basic versioning, the difference between authoring tools or creator applications, nuances between things like upload, catalog, and ingest, another book in the NAB Executive Technology Briefing series: *Digital Content Management: Creating and Distributing Media Assets by Broadcasters* by Joan Van Tassel is a great resource. Even more good references for more detail on industry terms are listed in the resources section at the end of this book.

As the future system, processes, and practices are defined, the following list of topics may serve as a guideline:

System Definition

- Use cases for user groups and roles

- File types

- Structured versus unstructured content

- Content flow

- Application Design

- UI (user interface) requirements

- System architecture (discussed in detail in Chapters 7 and 8)

- User/security administration

- Business Process Integration

- Workflow or business process automation

- Assembly and manipulation tools

System Definition

To begin with, the users of the system must be identified and their roles relative to the system be defined.

Use Cases for User Groups and Roles

The implementation team should spend quality time with new users and administrators in order to define what it is exactly that they do and how the system expansion will affect that routine. These discussions should yield new, potentially interconnected but clearly separated, use cases for different roles. It is not necessary to be fully detailed at this stage, but this information should start to foster the idea of use case templates to assist throughout the implementation phase with requirements definition, product specs and configuration, and ultimately, with training. One guiding thought behind this should be to distinguish use cases that can be logically grouped together for implementation phases.

Users who have common tasks and privileges should be defined in groups and roles. In most cases, each role will have its own use case. When defining user roles, it is advisable to include the levels of application security that must accompany them. See the section about System Security below. The roles will become clearer as the system expansion moves from planning into implementation but an initial assessment can be provided following the template example shown in Table 4.1.

Chapter 1 includes the recommendation for a detailed document that describes the existing system in comprehensive terms, and, possibly, a separate document that describes the how the organization got where it is. These documents should also include some current use cases detailing processes and workflow. These documents will provide a good example that can be used by the team involved in a vertical or horizontal expansion.

While use cases may not necessarily change for systems that simply scale in size, it is still a very good idea to extend some effort to plan the process in logical steps.

User Group: Photo Desk
User Role Title: Photo Desk Standard User
Description:
The Photo Desk Standard User will search and download content required to produce marketing material. Certain work products and the final form content will be uploaded back into the system.

ACTION	COMMENTS	REQUIREMENTS	FILE INFORMATION REQUIRED
Search images, line art and graphics by category, and sub category keywords, byline, or story title. Examine Search results and download images.	Search images, line art and graphics is the most frequent activity of this role in the system.	Low res thumbnail in search result display for identification, enlargement view for closer inspection and high resolution (300dpi) full size image for download. Users in this role should be able to download images directly into Adobe Photoshop and line art into Adobe Illustrator.	Color space, File Size. File Type, Resolution, Usage Rights
Search video clips by category, and sub category, file name, story title Identify and view stories, and download file or individual stills	The Photo Desk sometimes uses video stills if no other images are available.	Animated thumbnail for identification and an option to view a web stream and download or order high resolution or still of specific frames. In addition, a tabulated list view is essential, showing search results with story title, air date/time and any applicable usage restrictions.	Show that used story, Producer Name, ...

ACTION	COMMENTS	REQUIREMENTS	FILE INFORMATION REQUIRED
Upload images and line art and provide basic metadata: File Name, Title, Creator. Images are associated with the correct category.	After images have been prepared they are uploaded into the corresponding category. For the naming convention, see Photo Desk naming convention document. Images are associated with the correct campaign and product category.	Ideally users in this role should be able to upload and provide metadata and category assignments directly from Adobe Photoshop and line art from Adobe Illustrator. (IPTC)	

TABLE 4.1 *Use Case Template*

Use cases are sometimes also referred to as use scenarios. They usually focus on a specific role. They should provide a definition of that role and describe how users of that role will interact with the system. Table 4.1 is a use case example. It is not required to provide all details in the initial stage of a project. The key elements are the role description and the actions taken by that role:

File Types

If assuming the expansion will handle file types that the existing system does not handle; one may also need to define the new types of files. Many times, organizations do not have a unified view and understanding of the file types in use. For example, the way different users describe photos, images, or stock art is often different. Video files are equally complex because the encoding type and quality can vary as much as the variability in photographs and stock art. Therefore, it may be helpful to start with a matrix that includes more technical definitions of the terms used in the organization, such as in Table 4.2.

A matrix should accomplish a few things:

• Clarify for the project participants and the vendor what file types are in use, and how they relate to the use cases defined.

• Point to the technology a vendor will need to bring to the table to create or extract useful representations of the files (visual thumbnails and proxies, or textual summaries or keywords for example).

STOCK ART, HIGH RES IMAGES	300 DPI JPEG	USED BY ART BUYER (STOCK ART) AND STUDIO (HIGH RES IMAGES)
Stock Art, High Res Images	300 dpi JPEG	Used by Art Buyer (Stock Art) and Studio (High Res Images)
Low Res Images	150 or 72 dpi JPEG	Low Res duplicates of Stock Art used by Studio
Native Images	Photoshop EPS files of different resolutions	Created and used by Studio
Composite Image	JPEG or Photoshop EPS files of different resolutions	Created by Studio when combining multiple images into one

TABLE 4.2 *Sample File Matrix for Images*

- Provide information to the team and the vendor regarding the organization of files and file categories. This will also help define the required metadata templates.

- Determine what kinds of file transformations/manipulations are common in the organization.

- Clearly identifying file types is especially important when planning to include rich media files in the use cases. Rich media files are typically those that are visual in nature, including images, video, design documents (brochures, posters), animations (Flash), 3D models, and so on.

Rich media file management is most commonly referred to as digital asset management or DAM. DAM vendors will most likely refer to file types by their mime type. Here is a link with more detail on mime types for the curious reader: http://www.juicystudio.com/tutorial/xhtml/mime.asp#mimetypes

Structured Versus Unstructured Content

An additional categorization of file types is that of structured versus unstructured content. Defining this distinction is important specifically for systems that will manage mostly text-based content (e.g., Web content and documents management systems) because structured content can often be subdivided into smaller reusable elements or components, in effect separating content and format. For example, by clearly identifying the summary at the beginning of a press release, this section of the text can be used to represent the text on Web sites that display the summary of all the available press releases. Thus, components of one document can serve multiple purposes in different formats without the need to edit or recreate them. The list of examples below should help to determine if the area of structured data is something that needs further exploration.

STRUCTURED OR TEMPLATE-BASED CONTENT	UNSTRUCTURED CONTENT
Records and statements (e.g., financial or utilities)	Images or photos
Template documents (e.g., manuals, policies, and such)	Drawings (e.g., Adobe Illustrator, MSVisio)
Correspondence (e.g., faxes, e-mails, letters)	Logos
Statements and press releases	Fonts
	Design Documents (e.g., QuarkXPress, InDesign, and more)
	Power Point

	Time-Based Media
	    Video
	    Audio
	    Animations (e.g., Flash)

If there is a large amount of text-based information that can be subdivided in reusable sections and these sections are consistent across this type of content, they can be managed using technologies and processes that allow defining and identifying the reusable components in the repository. The optimal format to represent structured documents is extended markup language (XML) in some cases in combination with a document type definition (DTD). XML-based systems are readily available today. Defining the smallest reusable component of information is further explained in publications focusing on document and web content management.

Some content could fall under either category depending on the ability of the system to consistently identify components within a document.

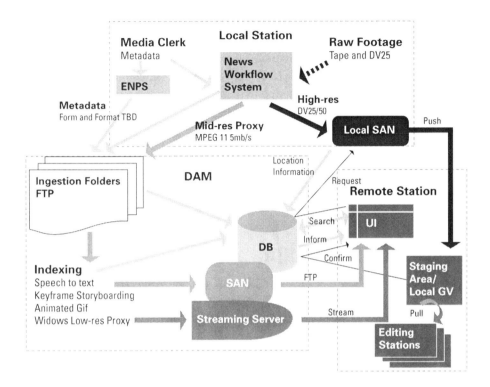

FIGURE 4.1 *Sample Content Flowchart*

Content Flow

With the combination of use cases, user roles, and file types, the flow of assets through the organization can now be defined with some degree of technical detail.

In planning the timeline for the system expansion, consider spending a significant amount of time defining the taxonomy for the new file types and what changes may be required for the existing taxonomy. Taxonomy tends to be an underestimated element of many content management systems. For that reason, the Chapters 10 and 11 are devoted to that topic.

At this point, one should be able to create flow charts and use cases that outline who needs access to what content. The charts should include exact technical descriptions in terms of file types, resolution, format, and so on, as well as the flow of file information or metadata. An example is shown in Figure 4.1.

When creating these flow charts, it is important to step back and reapply the phased methodology approach. If a flow chart is becoming too complex to comprehend in a simple meeting, consider breaking it down into smaller pieces. Establishing simple, logical blocks that can translate into implementation phases is the key to a successful implementation. Take care not to over-engineer the process. Don't forget to use common sense. Automated processes are not always necessary. Traditional channels such as e-mail, phone, and walking down the hall can be the best way to accomplish certain steps and use cases.

The well-defined building blocks of the envisioned system should now provide sufficient information for a vendor or integrator to provide the organization with implementation designs and price quotes. However, there are still a few more things to consider in planning the system expansion and making the vendor selection.

Application Design

After defining who the users are and how the content needs to be accessed and moved though the system, it is now necessary to consider the functional and technical requirements of the core digital content management system.

User Interface (UI) Requirements

The benchmark for a successful implementation is the representation of information to the user and administrator and the ease with which a user finds what he or she wants. How well the system accomplishes these key elements is determined in large part by the quality of UI design.

Most user interfaces (but not necessarily all admininstrator interfaces) are Web-based. This has the advantage that anyone with a computer and network access can get to the application. Almost every computer has a Web browser. No special software has to be installed and maintained. However, it has also some disadvantages. Web browsers are relatively "dumb" in comparison to special software installed on a computer. Interface designers must attempt to overcome any technical limitations of the Web browser as much as possible.

The complexity of Web application design should not be underestimated. A Web site used to be a relatively simple thing but now, a Web application or, more exactly, an application that is accessed through a Web browser, can be extremely complex. In many cases, moving a single element from one page to another is not as easy as it looks to the untrained eye.

If this complexity is coupled with proprietary code that limits the UI design options, this may present a big issue. As will be described in Chapter 8, the separation between the application and the presentation becomes more and more important as the system grows either vertically or horizontally.

While working with the vendor on the final UI design for the system, some decisions need to be made. When building the use cases, it needs to be defined what metadata users will see in the interface for each given file type. Depending on the use case, the metadata displayed can vary even for the same file type. For example, most users will only need to see a subset of all available metadata, and the data that is available may also depend on the function a user is asked to perform on a given screen: search, view, download, or edit.

In a larger system, not all users are equally well served by the same interface. Brower-based interfaces can be part of an existing intranet or extranet, or they can be dedicated to specific clients or departments within or outside of the organization. Flexible, open standards-based UI frameworks make it easier for the average-skilled HTML programmer to build ad hoc interfaces, if necessary.

Another important reason to consider creating multiple interfaces is to provide accessibility to users who speak different languages. Searching and operating a system in multiple languages adds a degree of complexity that has to be planned for in UI design, taxonomy, and the business case. This issue is examined further in Chapters 6 and 7 dedicated to the business case and in Chapters 10 and 11, which are focused on the taxonomy considerations of system expansions.

System Architecture

It is crucial to work closely with the vendor(s) or integrator when it comes to the system architecture. However, there are a few key attributes that a larger content management system should provide. The vendor selection should take these into account. Chapter 8 details important considerations for hardware and software, and Chapter 9 describes advanced integration approaches. Here, it should suffice that a true enterprise system will be able to expand in all three ways: in size, vertically, and horizontally.

System Security

Detailed recommendations for building the structure of user roles and groups and the associated security cannot be made without knowing the business case. However, it is likely that in a larger system, one will have to consider complex workflows that require a well thought through system of permissions and privileges. Below are a few concepts that need to be considered when expanding from a focused vertical solution to a larger horizontal enterprise strategy. Security models for larger interlocking systems can become very complex, and it might be well worth to work with independent consultants who can draw on specific experience in this field.

Privileges and Permissions

The distinction between privileges and permissions is common knowledge for system administrators of larger IT networks, but it might be new to the business owner of a content management system. Privileges define what users or user groups can do (read, edit, delete, download, version, and such). Permissions are assigned to the file or asset or any grouping of content. Permissions define what users or user groups are allowed to do with those assets. It is the combination of what a user *can* do and what a user is *allowed* to do that ultimately governs the rules.

Intersecting Permissions

In some cases it is not the combination of privileges and permissions that should define who can do what with an asset or group of assets. A business might have the case of Brand A and Model B. Users might be able to see (read) all Brand A assets but only are allowed to edit if those assets are also contained with the set of assets that are common to Model B. It is the intersection of two group assignments that should rule the permission set.

While this is complex, it is possible to define rules such as these in the best enterprise systems. Remember, again, that true enterprise applications are not necessarily the most feature-rich out-of-the-box. It is their expandability that makes the difference. Building complex security models that perform complex searches in milliseconds is the fine art of high-end enterprise content management systems. Additional implications of the user security are discussed in Chapter 11.

Application Security versus UI Filters

Depending on the circumstances, one might find that building complex security models is not possible in either the current or preferred system. As mentioned before, the flexibility of the presentation layer or UI can become very useful in that case. Here is one example:

A brand portal for a consumer goods company might have a separate interface for each brand. This allows for easy navigation as well as for UI filters. Simply accessing the system through a specific interface will restrict access to assets of a certain brand and, potentially, to certain actions with in that interface.

The downside to UI filters is that they can have a devastating effect on performance, and that they often rely on sending URLs that can be much easier to "hack" than the security of the core application. For highly security-sensitive material, this might not be an option. For marketing materials this is usually not an issue.

Lightweight Directory Access Protocol (LDAP)

As users are assigned to a certain level of permissions and privileges, it will be necessary to identify users at the time they interact with the digital content management system. User will have to log on by providing a User ID and Password. This process, also called authentication, requires that the login information or credential of the users are stored somewhere. In smaller systems that information can be part of the user record in the database that will have to be entered and maintained by an application administrator. To avoid maintaining the user credentials for various systems in parallel, many IT organizations use LDAP-based authentication. In this case the user credentials are stored and administered in only one location. If a user logs on to the system the credentials are sent to the LDAP server for authentication. Upon positive conformation the user is allowed access to the specific application they logged into.

> There are different flavors of LDAP. One is an open standard administer by the Open LDAP Group which can be found at http://www.openldap.org. The two predominant products are iPlanet, Microsoft Active Directory.

Single Sign On (SSO)

SSO is taking the concept of simplifying the authentication process a step further. In most organizations users have a user ID and password that is used when logging into the computer at work or into the company intra or extranets. The concept of SSO is that the credentials of the initial authentication can be stored for a set period of time and when a user requests access to a specific system (i.e. The content management system) the same credentials are reused without the user having to provide them again. The authentication process is transparent to the user. If a positive confirmation conformation is received the user can access the system with a click of a button. Both LDAP and SSO will however not eliminate the need for thorough application security design and maintenance. The permission level for user roles and complex issues like intersecting permissions are still managed within the content management system. Only the basic authentication and the high level role assignment of the users are usually managed by LDAP and SSO systems.

Business Process Integration

As the final step in the process, integration of the new content management system with the business processes needs to be defined. Some functionality may be part of the core system, while other elements may be provided by additional tools or plugins.

Workflow or Business Process Automation

One will find that there are many rules that define who can do what and, also, when. This leads to the topic of workflow or business process automation. The core of any system is a well-defined repository of all of the content. The permissions and privileges define who can do what with the assets. However, assets do not remain static. They need to move through steps and be assembled, edited, versioned, approved, or rejected, and, at some point, distributed to end users or production facilities for physical production (print, for example).

Many vendors offer some degree of business process automation as an integrated package with their solutions. In some cases the separation of repository and workflow is not obvious at all. This issue and its implications on expanding a content management system are described in Chapter 8. Here it suffices to say that connecting the hubs that make up the life cycle of the assets in a vertical expansion should be planned as outlined above, handling one use case and one logical block at a time as illustrated in Figure 4.2.

Below are a few points to assist in planning:

- **Metadata-driven Security:** Some workflows can be driven by administrative metadata alone. The security model might allow users to see only assets of a certain status. That status can be part of the metadata. Users can only see assets if the status allows them to do so.

- **Saved Searches:** If a system allows for saved searches, the administrator can create predefined searches that specify parameters relevant to the workflow. For example: Status = Not Reviewed AND Brand = MyBrand. The users in charge of a task can access those saved searches through a simple click of a button. In this example, that would be the users responsible for reviewing MyBrand assets.

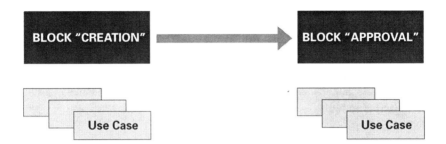

FIGURE 4.2 *Defining Use Cases in Blocks of Activity*

- **Scheduling:** More sophisticated workflows will need scheduling options for starting and completion dates of tasks.

- **Notification:** The system may need the ability to send notifications to users or administrators, signaling new, completed, or overdue tasks. Be sure to work with the users and administrators to define what notifications are truly important. Be cognizant also of the number of e-mails this might create.

- **Rules:** More complex workflows may have time-based and other rules (if no decision by X date, then do this...).

- **Serial or Parallel Workflow:** Is a serial or parallel workflow a better fit? Legal and design review might run in parallel, but distribution always follows approval, and therefore represents a serial workflow.

- **Tracking and Reporting:** Consider the need to trace and report data from the workflow. For example, one might want to know who approved what and when. Be sure the system can be configured to get the reporting that is needed.

Assembly and Manipulation Tools

The ability to assemble content in a certain order or to manipulate it to some degree might be important to the organization. For example, a user might need to assemble a few video clips in a certain order and add audio files. In other cases markup and annotation of a brochure in the review process might be an objective. It is obvious that these elements vary significantly from vertical to vertical and some times even within different stages of one life cycle.

Again, the goal is to end up with a well-defined set of requirements with regard to the workflow and to allow vendors to quote against those specified requirements before making the final decision.

Specifically, in a horizontal expansion of a system, one will find that "solution vendors" will have a hard time providing workflow solutions that are flexible enough to model the flow of XML-based product documentation processes or to handle print as well as they handle video workflows. Vertical solutions may meet the requirements better. Chapter 9 takes a closer look at integration also of assembly and manipulation tools.

Summary

This chapter has provided some structure to the concepts and planning process. Many aspects of system expansion can be planned and even defined before making a vendor or technology decision. A very common mistake is to pick a vendor too early and rely too heavily on "the fox to build the hen house."

The larger the system and the more forward thinking the strategy, the more important it is that, with the help of truly unbiased advice, the user/planner drives the strategy and implementation projects. Just as in building a house, it is advisable to seek advice from an architect and an engineer and, potentially, an interior designer to define what one needs and what one wants. Only after arriving at a detailed concept, should bids from the contractor be solicited.

5 Digital Rights Management, Authentication, and Compliance

Digital rights management (DRM), authentication, and compliance are three related areas that have become a key concern in many organizations dealing with digital content. These topics encompass areas like copyright and usage rights restriction, the enforcement thereof, and authentication of content (did it really come from this repository and was it meant for this use?). There is much to be said about DRM, this technology has become its own niche industry. This chapter discusses a few areas that might help to structure thoughts and requirements around rights and restrictions inside and outside of the system. More research might be necessary for defining the final approach. The resource section at the end of this chapter will provide additional sources of information about the topics discussed here.

There are several areas that come into play when discussing rights management issues as they relate to content management systems:

- Management of the contracts, agreements, and licenses that govern the usage rights of content

- Tracking and linking of the rights information with the content

- Tracking the use of content for reporting and compliance

- Enforcement of usage rights restriction

> In addition, there are some issues that are not directly related to content management, but anyone considering an integrated solution should examine them none the less. These include the management of payable and receivable royalty and license payments, general policies for negotiating usage rights with rights owners such as freelancers, contractors, or stock houses, and policies for granting rights for use of content to consumers and businesses. These issues are important as an enterprise-wide approach to digital content management will most likely require rethinking and restructuring in these areas. These issues, however, are outside the scope of this book, but the resource section references some excellent books and articles on these topics.

Managing the contracts, agreements, and licenses that govern the usage rights of content is part of the broader topic of contract management. This topic has been well researched by many organizations, and contract management solutions are provided by many document management companies. There is even an organization dedicated to the topic. The National Contract Management Association (http://www.ncmahq.org/) can provide additional information and recommendations, as well as best practices.

This chapter will focus on the less understood topics of defining, tracking, and enforcing of usage rights restrictions in the digital content management system.

Defining, Tracking, and Enforcing Usage Rights Restrictions

When considering the definition and tracking of usage rights, there are two areas to think about. First, is the ability of the repository to manage access to content depending on the legal rights and restrictions that affect that content. Second, is to define what happens to content after it leaves the system via download, email, or burned on a CD/DVD.

Tracking Rights and Restrictions within the System

Many organizations are just starting to define those rights and restrictions. One way to do this is with the file-type matrix discussed in Chapter 4. Any file type that has any kind of usage rights restriction such as a copyright for a photographer or author, for example, should be marked.

MEDIA TYPE/ GEOGRAPHY	NORTH AMERICA	EU	...	ALL
Newspaper	North America Print	EU Newspaper		Global Newspaper
Magazines	North America Print	EU Magazine		Global Magazine
Web Internal	Web Internal	Web Internal		Web Internal
Web External	North America Web External	EU Web External		Global Web External

TABLE 5.1 *Sample Rights Matrix*

Some organizations have different rights and restrictions that can be refined to media types and geographic areas, for example. To ensure that all project participants use the same term to describe the same type of right or restriction, consider creating very clear definitions of the restriction type. In an example of media type and geography restrictions, a matrix approach, as shown in Table 5.1, can work well. The defined terms will become the metadata indicators for the usage rights.

No matter if the rights model is simple or complex, one will most likely have to also consider the expiration date of those rights. The system should allow for defining multiple expiration dates (for example: North America Print 02.15.08 but also EU Newspaper 02.15.07).

Using this matrix, the vendor should now be able to tell what it will take to enforce these rights and restrictions in the system of choice. In general, there are a few options for what to do when a file expires. Here are few examples:

- Notify the administrator of approaching expiration dates

- Delete the files if all rights have expired

- Pull the files from available distribution but leave them in the system for repurchase by an administrator or art buyer

- Pull native files from distribution but leave a watermarked low resolution or sample in distribution for reorder

In many cases, one also needs to make sure that any content that might contain an expired element is located and handled accordingly. A photo might have been used in a poster or an article might have been used in a different document or Web site. If these rights must be tracked as well, the system needs to be able to track the relationship between the original content and any reuse of it.

Tracking Files After They Leave the System

Obviously, it is not as easy to make sure a file is not used in a certain way after it has left the system. For example, a user might reuse a rights protected file that was legally downloaded a few months back but the rights have expired by now. These kinds of reuse practices inadvertently open the organization up to the risk of legal action by a copyright owner.

It is important to do what is possible to ensure that the system's users follow certain processes. One process recommendation would be never to save files for reuse on a personal hard drive and always use the system to obtain the most current version. If defining strict processes is not satisfying the organization's need for control over its content, then a look into new DRM technology may be worthwhile.

DRM Technology

DRM provides options today that will prevent misuse more effectively than any process recommendation could do in the past. Besides adding visible watermarks to expired files, systems can also add invisible watermarks that are like smart chips. Each time a file and, in some cases, renditions of that file touch the Internet cloud, it "calls home" and "reports" its use. If the file's ID is determined to be that of an expired file, a notification can be sent to warn of possible misuse. In addition, the system can use sniffer or crawler programs that search the Internet for predefined IDs. If they find those identifiers, they call home with the location of the file.

In regard to music and film, enforcing rights is often tied to the media and the operating system or player applications. In that regard, Microsoft Media Player, as well as Real and Quick Time Players are working on rights-enforcing technology.

Another effort is underway in the area of CD/DVD rights enforcement. Blue-Ray Disc and HD-DVD are new formats for DVDs that are marketed as more compact data storage and playback mediums. A blue-ray disc is supposedly able to hold between 25GB and 54GB. But besides discs holding more data, the consortiums that are leading the parallel efforts are also interested in making rights enforcement easier.[1]

---

1. Blue-Ray Disc Association, http://www.bluraydisc.com/ and the HD-DVD Promotion Group http://www.hddvdprg.com

Authentication

Adobe has made great strides in authentication options for PDF documents. Please contact Adobe (www.adobe.com) for more information (2).

Various native file types such as .tif or .eps images, video, and sometimes even .txt or XML files are not covered by the .pdf approach. However, these files can be authenticated using a similar approach to the watermark method described above. Tools can include a unique identifier in any file that leaves the system. These identifiers can be used to authenticate files, for example, by simple "drag and drop" onto a specified website (for example: www.company-name.com/authentication). If a user drags and drops a file onto the designated authentication site, the unique ID is sent to the system and collects some useful metadata such as the original file name, file type, expiration date, author, print buyer, and so on. This information can be helpful not only in preventing accidental misuse, but it can also confirm that a file did indeed come from a specific repository. The system should even be able to track when the file was downloaded and by whom.

While these technologies are available today, they are not inexpensive, and in addition to the cost of the technology, one will need to plan for some level of integration with the system.

Compliance

Depending on industry, legal compliance may be an issue. There are many different compliance laws (HIPPA, Sarbanes-Oxley, and many more). In general, compliance will cover one or more of the following cases:

Requirement to Produce a Record or Records

In this case a company may be required to produce a record (policy, email, or other document) in a set time frame. For example, a judge orders a company to provide all emails with one or more of the following criteria to be presented by a fixed deadline:

- A certain subject
- From or to a certain individual
- With a specific word or phrase in the body of the email
- For a certain time period

- In some cases, companies have just a few days to produce the complete set of records or documents or face a hefty fine.

> The Sarbanes-Oxley law (SOX) states that all communication regarding the creation of financial statements needs to be made available. It is not entirely clear what exactly is meant by "all" in this case, as one will not record every water cooler discussion or meeting. It is fair to assume it means all documents or files that are available, including email and also instant messages (IM), if the company uses that tool.

Any good content management system should be able to find a specific document or documents relating to a specific topic. However, the company might have to ensure that nothing was deleted. In more sophisticated document management or digital asset management systems, this can be set through asset permissions.

Another way of enforcing that a digital asset or record is not deleted is to control deletion at the hardware level. Write once read many (WORM) storage technology is common infrastructure for records management in many financial or health care organizations. This technology prevents any deletion or editing of files. Any edit has to be in the form of a new version.

Requirement to Provide a Certain Version and Metadata of a Record

Where emails have threads, other content has versions. The company might be required to prove that a user who searched at a given time found a certain version of a document (policy or procedure, for example).

The same issue regarding deletion also applies in this case; it can be controlled, and it can be limited in terms of who can and cannot delete items. In addition, the system will need to be able to keep any version of a document or record and also track the exact date and time those versions were created. Version tracking is a common feature in most content management systems. However, this might not be enough. For example, a user might claim that he typed a specific number or search term into a browser-based access page. If these search terms are searching against metadata values, one might have to prove that the metadata used to find that document or record had the correct value at that time. The system needs to be able also to track metadata versioning to ensure proof that a search for a certain term at a certain time would have found the correct record or document.

The same is true if metadata was displayed as additional information with the record or document. For example, the security status of a document might be part of the metadata record. In that case one might have to prove that the status value was set correctly at a certain time.

Requirement for Access Security

In some cases one will need to prove that the application security can limit access to certain documents and records to a certain audience, and that this access control is tamper-proof.

Requirement to Prove Who Accessed a Record or Document and When (Usage Tracking)

The company might need to be able to prove who accessed a record and when that individual accessed it. For that, the system needs to be able to do two things: manage user accounts, including tracking any privilege changes to that user account, and track any view or download transaction of the content by that user.

A user must authenticate in some way so that it can be proven later who accessed the system. If the system can track both viewing and downloading of its content, there should be no problem producing the required information as long as the user ID is part of the transaction record.

The catch is the view transaction. Most systems track download transactions, but not all track a simple view of an asset or record. In this case, one might have to limit the display to document summaries and force a user to download or order the content if he wishes to view the full document or record.

> However, the issue might not stop here. If dealing with security-sensitive material or copyrights, tracking content after it has left the system becomes an issue. Even if the view transaction can be tracked, it is important to consider that any standard browser can take a screen shot of the information that is displayed. That screen shot can be emailed or printed. Therefore, the ability to track view transactions might not eliminate the problem. The issue of tracking content outside of the system was addressed earlier in this chapter in the section "Tracking files after they leave the system."

Highly security-sensitive or classified material is best managed with old-style security measures. Only certain computers that specifically do not allow taking a screen shot, email, or print, and that might not be connected to the Internet, will display the information as view-only. Readers might remember the old blue-screen monitors, some of which are still in use at local libraries. This is the same concept. In this case, the user interface is probably not browser-based, but rather is a proprietary client-side application.

Case Study

Corbis

Background

Corbis is a Seattle-based provider of stock photography, illustration, motion and fine art. By 1999, Corbis had moved a large portion of its collection to the Web and began licensing images online. By opening up its collection to the public and making it easily accessible over the Web, Corbis was meeting the business needs of its customers. But it also faced the risk of images being downloaded from its site and used without a license or authorization. Between 2000 and 2001, Corbis' online business had increased significantly. At the same time, the company began to see an increase in infringement activity. Infringements ranged from low-resolution images being taken off the Corbis site or CDs and posted elsewhere to images that are only licensed for one use, such as the Web, showing up in catalogs, ads, or other media. Corbis identified several goals for a content management system:

Business Goal

- Make it easier and more cost effective for Corbis' customers to lawfully use images
- Protect the rights of Corbis' media providers and photographers
- Correct misuse of Corbis images

Technical Goal

- Embed unique IDs within millions of digital images that facilitate copyright and license compliance
- Track Corbis-distributed images on the Web to identify licensing opportunities and potential infringement issues

Solution

To address the problem of infringement and to make it easy for customers to license images, Corbis implemented a copyright protection program that CONTINUED ▶

CONTINUED ▶ combines copyright registration, image tracking, and a compliance licensing program. In addition, Corbis employs a legal team dedicated to investigating reports of infringement, determining which cases to pursue, and using both business and legal remedies to recover revenue. Corbis continues to believe that providing a structured program designed to protect the valuable assets it represents is critical to its business. To that end, Corbis has developed a sophisticated policing program aimed at reducing instances of infringement.

Digital watermarking has proven to offer one of the most reliable image tracking systems on the Web. And digital watermarking is complementary to other digital rights management and image tagging techniques, making it compatible with Corbis' evolving workflows.

As a result, Corbis was an early adopter of Digimarc digital watermarking solutions, using the technology as early as 1996 to add a unique image ID to images as a means to communicate copyright and facilitate license compliance, and to track those images as they were distributed digitally. Today, Corbis continues to rely on Digimarc to provide actionable data that helps to identify and prioritizes case where Corbis' action is required.

As part of its digital distribution strategy, Corbis uses Digimarc ImageBridge™ watermarking to place imperceptible digital watermarks carrying a unique image ID into millions of the images displayed on www.corbis.com. It also employs Digimarc MarcSpider™ image tracking as a means to search the public Internet for its images, feeding Corbis' rights management and compliance program.

Result

Since the time Corbis made a strategic business decision to move its image collection to the Web, Digimarc solutions have become the cornerstone of Corbis' copyright protection program.

As its Internet business has grown, so have the number of identified infringements. The Digimarc MarcSpider service examines more than 50 million images a month and generates a report of both legitimate and potentially infringing uses of images, making it easier for Corbis to manage image assets and enable compliance. Today, Corbis identifies dozens of cases of potentially unauthorized use of Corbis images per month using Digimarc digital watermarking solutions. Policing these cases enables Corbis to recover compliance revenue that would otherwise be lost – in 2005 this revenue was estimated to be well over $1 million.

Published with the permission of Corbis and Digimarc

Summary

Digital rights management, authentication, and compliance are complex and multi-faceted aspects of digital content management. However, companies can start approaching these topics with some basic steps: identifying the rights and compliance related issues around the content they own and distribute, and defining the most effective ways of tracking usage rights or compliance-related data. More complex and integrated solutions will require thorough research and analysis. New technologies in the area of digital rights enforcement are in development, and implementation strategies are best accomplished in phases. As with other aspects of an enterprise approach to digital content management, a successful strategy will be a flexible approach that brings together multiple technologies, products, and business practices.

6 Building the Business Case for a System Expansion

The underlying assumption for this book is that the planner and the organization have some degree of experience with digital content management. That experience, in combination with the issues raised in the prior chapters, should point to one clear concept: large-scale content management is not based on a tool or technology alone, but as much on processes, practices, and governance models that will represent a significant change to the business process of an organization. A broader approach for digital content management represents a significant strategic investment, not a purchase.

ROI and Business Goals

As with all enterprise-scale initiatives, any investment should follow a definition of a long-term business plan or vision and a well thought out implementation strategy. A surprising number of business cases are based on little more than a very rough return on investment (ROI) calculation. While in a smaller departmental project the business rationale for digital content management might be obvious from the ROI calculations alone, those calculations become more difficult for larger, interconnected systems.

In many cases, introducing digital repositories and workflows is a disruptive innovation that requires significant internal resources for planning, implementation, and change management. The importance of the internal tasks and governance of these initiatives was highlighted in previous chapters.

Many ROI calculations, especially those provided by product vendors, do not fully acknowledge all costs to the organization. At the same time they do not take into account the larger business objectives. The larger the system and the more interconnected the system will become; the more choices and tasks will be affecting the complexity of the project. In addition, market changes and technology innovation can extend significant pressure on organizations and force them to consider changes reaching the core of their business models. These external forces need to be considered in a long-term digital content management strategy.

While the business case for each implementation phase should include a ROI calculation, it is not the hard numbers alone that will ensure the implementations will eventually result in increased profitability and productivity. With the growing complexity of the project, it is increasingly important to have a very clear vision of the ultimate goal for the initiative. The business case for larger interconnected digital content management should therefore start with a clear definition of the overall strategic direction or vision. Once that is established, any ROI calculation can be assured of taking all components into consideration. ROI models are covered in depth in Chapter 7.

Vision, Strategy, and Profit: In that Order

There is an important difference in building a business vision and building a strategy. A vision should be a general goal. A vision is the process of building consensus about the overall direction of the organization. The strategy is the process of building consensus on the implementation phases, milestones, and measurements.

There are many trends that force companies to define new visions for their business. The most obvious and far reaching trends are:

- Offering more value-added services and/or establish new revenue streams

- Globalization

- Cost savings

- Regulations and compliance laws

The trend to service-oriented offerings across all industries continues to gain speed. A print shop, for instance, may offer online job submissions and asset management, many post-production houses offer digital order and trafficking solutions, and agencies become rich media managers for their clients. Many, if not most, of the new value-added service offerings include online and digital content. These services are designed as a competitive advantage or as a new source of revenue.

On the other hand, the global business environment continues to shift production away from the traditional manufacturing centers, and companies in the highly developed parts of the world are struggling to adopt. They are becoming brand owners and knowledge centers, while manufacturing and even service tasks are provided offshore. Knowledge, innovation, and brands combined are now the true assets. Intellectual property (IP) is the new currency. IP exists in the form of documents that describe processes, research, policies, and contracts, and, in increasing numbers, also rich media like advertisements, brochures, training videos, and more. However, few companies have truly adopted their organization to this new reality.

Other trends include the exponentially growing amount of new content created in organizations today and the increasing need to cut costs in markets with shrinking margins.

All these trends require large-scale visions and strategies for digital content management. An important step for any organization considering a larger content management strategy is to define a vision of how it sees itself in this changing business landscape. This vision is the guiding and unifying element that leads to the strategy which should be a combination of technology, processes, practices, and governance that should enable the organization to more efficiently, mange, distribute, control, and destroy content in order to fulfill the vision

Building the Strategy

As a first step in that process, an organization will have to define the motivating factor for engaging a larger content management strategy. It is usually one or a combination of these four aspects:

• New business opportunities (top line revenue)

• Efficiency gains (bottom line savings)

• Competitive advantage by expanding services (loss leader)

• Legal reasons due to compliance laws (i.e., Sarbanes-Oxley)

The outcome should be a mission statement clarifying the strategic objective that defines the unifying goal for all stakeholders. This vision and the resulting strategies should be built on a deep understanding of the internal and external business factors within the vertical market, as well as on increasing competency in the digital content management space. Educating all levels of the organization is key to growing awareness and competency in content management. Please refer to the executive summary at the beginning of this book for an overview of the digital content management industry.

Executive Strategy

With any larger initiative that has multiple cross-departmental elements, there should be at least two levels of planning. The senior executives that are responsible for the larger business vision will need to establish and agree upon the overall company strategy to implement this larger vision. On this level, the content management strategy needs to be aligned with other key business strategies such as mergers, acquisitions, globalization, centralization, decentralization, and so on. As phases with significant business impact and limited risk are defined, the planning can move to the mid-level managers who can then engage in the traditional business case development.

Another important aspect of building the larger strategy is that the strategy is not equal to the larger vision. The vision is the long-term goal that should remain fixed as much as possible. The strategy, while consistent, should not be rigid. Mergers and acquisitions might fall through, technologies change, and market opportunities can appear with little notice. The overall strategy needs to be adjusted to those outside influences. In addition, the implementation of the first phases will most likely result in new knowledge and possibilities that might influence the strategy from within. Distinguishing the goal from the strategy is therefore a key requirement for long-term success.

As mentioned above, it will fall to the executive level to define the larger project phases and the business priorities of those phases. Areas of significant business impact with limited risk can be defined using common sense and data from comparable projects in the same industry vertical. For example, the organization might want to focus its initial business case on a specific service offering or productivity enhancement.

It is possible to run an analysis for multiple projects in parallel. For example, the feasibility and ROI of a new services offering can be researched while a general classification project is underway (see the Chapter 10 about taxonomy for more on classification). However, the impact of thorough analysis on the organization should not be underestimated. It might therefore make good sense to start with one or a very limited number of parallel projects until the competency and experience of the organization has increased.

Project Strategies

Once those initial projects have been defined, the mid-level managers should start defining the business case with a thorough analysis of the current state. Prior chapters provided actionable suggestions for establishing a detailed picture of the existing processes and content flows through the organization. At this point, focus should be on how this part of the process will affect the business case. If the organization plans to engage in a larger content management strategy, the analysis and problem definition will become a significant project in itself. It needs to be budgeted and staffed accordingly. Involving industry experts and consultants will most likely provide better results.

Here is a summary of key elements for business analysis and problem definition:

- Describe and chart the existing processes in small logical steps or sections. Each step should be comprehensible without significant time or explanation. If the block becomes too complex, it is advisable to cut it into smaller steps (see Chapters 1 and 4 for more detail).

- Start organizing and categorizing the content of the organization (see Chapter 10 on taxonomy for more detail).

- Ensure that the resulting workflow descriptions and charts are reviewed by the staff involved with those steps for their feedback and to build ownership.

- Resist the tendency to define solutions instead of problems. At this stage the question is not: "How can I make or do this better? "All focus should be on the question, "Am I describing the real problem or a symptom?"

- When defining outages and business problems, remember to focus on the larger vision.

Following these suggestions should result in a detailed but comprehensive document about the current state of the organization with regard to the defined implementation phase. The next step is to define the processes or best practices and create requirements documents or RFI/RFPs (request for information/proposal) if new technology is required.

Developing Process Recommendations and Technology Requirements

The analysis described above, in combination with definitions and workflow charts described in the prior chapters, will provide the basis for internal change processes as well as potential technology purchases. Increased understanding of the internal shortfalls and education on the possibilities of technology and best practices will be the basis for the requirements definition and implementation strategies of the different phases. The key question in this part of the project is, "What new or changed processes, practices, and technologies are required to achieve the goal for this phase?" On that level, ROI calculations are becoming a key element of the planning process. The next chapter will focus on the common ROI models in digital content management.

Process recommendations can include simple changes, such as standardization of file types. Examples include the use of MPEG2 at a certain bit rate, screen size, and frame rate as a standard for digitally stored video, or specific process definitions for acquisition of artwork. Another important practice is that of naming conventions and establishing a classification system including descriptive information (metadata) that will make it easier to find and reuse content (see Chapter11 about metadata for more detail).

Technology requirements can include features and functionalities including but not limited to those described in Chapter 4. Requirements should include such aspects as scalability, fault tolerance, redundancy, and availability. The key for this part of the business plan is to define the important elements of the required technology before deciding on any specific vendor or approach. This topic is also discussed in detail in Chapter 4. The goal is to have a good picture of the existing processes and content flow, including the challenges and the advantages, and also to have some understanding of the available technologies before approaching vendors to fill the gaps.

As mentioned above, the process recommendations and technology enhancements should list also the cost benefit.

A very important difference between a standalone project and one that is part of a larger vision and strategy is that recommendations and requirements are always viewed from the standpoint of that larger vision. As discussed in Chapter 3, one might initially compromise on functionality to gain flexibility and scalability for future phases.

Risk Assessment

Finally, the business case should also include an assessment of the risks. In fact, an assessment of such sort should be completed on both the strategic and the project-specific levels. Project-specific risks can usually be qualified in some detail, for example, with a matrix as shown in Table 6.1.

DEFINED RISK	AFFECTED TASKS	IMPACT	COMMENTS
Schedule delay of software delivery	Project management Migration Testing …	Cost increase and schedule delay	The software modules required for integrating the new system with existing ordering module could be delayed.
System outage (bug or technical issue)	All system use	Significant cost and productivity impact	If a total system failure occurs, significant time has to be spent for manual completion of tasks.

TABLE 6.1 *Matrix View for Identified Project Risks*

Mitigating the risks and calculating the cost of the risks are two steps that can follow the first step, which is solely focused on identifying the risks. Calculating the cost will be discussed in the next chapter, and risk mitigation is a topic in Chapter 1.

Case Study

CanWest MediaWorks

Background

CanWest MediaWorks is a large Canadian media company that operates multiple national TV stations, national and local news papers and websites. The company faced the following business challenges:

- Traditional revenue streams from advertising and subscription are not keeping pace with growth expectations
- New content forms and formats are evolving rapidly
- Content consumption patterns are changing, requiring more on-demand delivery via traditional and new, more targeted channels
- Costs associated with traditional workflows are high
- Time-to-market and capital required for seizing new revenue opportunities do not allow for required agility.

Solution

The company engaged Infosys Technologies to support them in analyzing their options and in building the business case for a company-wide digital CONTINUED ▶

CONTINUED ▶ content strategy. The result of that process was multiple detailed requirements definition documents and ROI models for infrastructure, process adjustments, and technology solutions which defined a roadmap of clearly defined delivery phases that address the following objectives:

Strategic
- Have all content available to anyone, on any device, at any time.
- Repurpose content better, faster, and cheaper.
- Introduce workflow efficiencies around locating, retrieving, and repurposing content.
- Remove "vertical silos" barriers that exist today for company-wide access to digital content
- Improve quality of content used and reduce both legal and expense exposure from using content obtained from third parties
- Gain competency in digital asset management and infrastructure sufficient to add value to current subscribers and seize opportunities for growth in traditional and new media markets and distribution channels
- Establish organizational competency in sharing content across the enterprise – shift workflow focus from "projects" to "process"
- Improve IT infrastructure to support company-wide integration of core services and content stores in highly secure and redundant locations.

Tactical
- Focus on fundamental systems to manage company's core content
- Ensure projects achieve immediate cost savings and process improvements for primary stakeholders
- Ensure process changes leverage existing competencies and mitigate production workflows disruptions
- Ensure projects are synchronized and support other in-progress or planned technology deployments and organizational changes

Result

CanWest Media Works is now working on the implementation of this strategy. In the first six months, the company aims to:
- Achieve operational cost savings (estimated at $300,000 per year from phase one)
- Support new business opportunities in non-traditional media distribution channels
- Improve content management related processes (metadata management)
- Enhance organizational competency in regards to company-wide content management
- Build trust and buy-in with users and stakeholders

Summary

To summarize, any successful implementation of a larger digital content management strategy must be tied to a larger business vision. Simply identifying business challenges on the departmental level without taking into account the larger business objectives can become a very costly way of implementing change. The business case for large-scale digital content management should be part of the strategic business plan and should include:

On the executive level

- Clear vision of the overall positioning

- Analysis of external business drivers

On the project level:

- Analysis of internal outages and enhancement options in regard to efficiency and/or revenue

- Recommendation for process change and technology solutions

- Risk assessment

- Calculation of the ROI

Building a business culture that aligns with a company's new strategies and business objectives is a key component in any larger change effort. However, the long-term success of the effort will require strong focus on building competency within the organization. Senior executives will need to build and embrace a strong vision that will lead the organization, specifically the implementation teams, through the unavoidable mistakes and tribulations.

CONTINUED ▶

7 ROI Models

Return on investment (ROI) is, of course, the ultimate goal of any business initiative. Returns on a content management project can be tangible and/or intangible and can manifest in many ways such as gained revenue, saved expenses, increased brand awareness, or compliance with regulatory guidelines. ROI calculations are a tool often used to build a business case. Unfortunately, this tool is often misused when people simplify the calculations and omit key expenditures, thus resulting in unrealistic expectations.

This chapter takes an honest look at the mistakes made in many calculations and provides hands-on suggestions for more complete and useful estimates on both investment and return of larger digital content management initiatives.

Calculating ROI

There are different methods to calculate ROI. The best overview of the methods the author has seen is the following text, published here with the permission of Joel Warwick.

ROI Methods

Published with permission from Joel Warwick, Content Management Strategy Consultant, San Rafael, CA.

CONTINUED ▶

CONTINUED ▶

Method A: Activity-task based, bottom-up model

This approach seeks to detail and measure the primary labor activities that benefit most from the technology. Essentially, before and after cost computations are applied to specific tasks. Cost savings from labor and material savings are computed, and time-to-market estimations can also be derived.

How It Works

This model consists of identifying key activities that will most benefit from the technology and that are conducted most frequently by the organization. Examples of these activities are searching the archive for previously broadcast content to reuse or researching a new story in development by viewing existing content in the archive. Time and cost data is then assigned to each task in each activity using any existing metrics the organization maintains and/or internal process knowledge and standards. The overall effect of these models is then calculated based on the frequency by which each activity occurs in a given period of time.

Advantages:

- It is very straightforward and tangible because it is built directly upon the actual tasks people perform.
- It is often accepted by key stakeholders and decision makers if the aggregate gains show a breakeven or better.
- If a net gain can be achieved through automating and optimizing just a handful of activities, then all other gains are icing on the cake, so to speak.
- Decision makers also often appreciate a more detailed analysis rather than an all-encompassing but relatively questionable financial model, described as Model B below, which is based on a number of assumptions.

Disadvantages:

CFOs and finance-oriented decision makers often expect and seek more traditional ROI metrics such as Net Present Value (NPV), Internal Rate of Return (IRR) or Total Cost of Ownership (TCO) that agree with the "top-down" numbers they maintain and use in their everyday operations.

The view provided by this method may provide an incomplete picture and subsequently places the burden on finance or IT to develop a more complete model to gauge the financial effect of system deployments.

Table A.1 in the appendix shows an example of a full bottom-up model spread sheet.

CONTINUED ▶

CONTINUED ▶

Method B: Top-down, traditional ROI calculation
How it works:

This model calculates the effect of a system deployment on the total expenditures related to its area of use. Models typically start with an overall expenditure number for a department or division and hone the number down using multiple filters to achieve a figure that represents the expenditures that could possibly be affected by this technology. This filtering is typically based on identifying and weighting the primary areas of roles, processes, and system functions that will most benefit or affect the portion of expenditures to which they are most related. Industry benchmarks are then applied to the final expenditure figure to determine the actual estimated savings that will be realized.

Advantages:

- These models appeal to finance personnel and senior decision makers as they result in traditional ROI calculations (NPV, IRR, TCO, etc.).
- The initial figures used often match and therefore appear to offer the same level of accuracy and synchronization to the sources from which they were initially derived (i.e., finance and accounting).
- These models allow finance teams to more easily leverage this data to prepare budgets, P&Ls, and other financial tools.

Disadvantages:

- This model doesn't not readily allow a drill-down to a tangible level where the actual functional benefits of a system become visible.
- Decision makers often can't correlate the operational benefits of the system to where in the financial models these benefits appear.
- Table A.2 in the appendix shows an example of a full top down model spread sheet.

Method C: Hybrid approach
How it works:

This model involves aspects of both models above and some level of reconciliation between them. In general, this approach is more difficult, as it requires bridging detailed activity data with high-level financial data. This method nearly always involves more work by the business case developers and a higher level of agreement between stakeholders. However, in cases where the direct, tangible benefits effectively prove the value of moving forward, but finance and executive sponsors require

CONTINUED ▶

CONTINUED ►

a comprehensive model that complies with technology funding and accounting practices already in place, this model can be effective. The underlying benefit and cost figures of this model are based on Method A above (activity/task-based). However a top-down model is created to complement the activity-based model and indicates the portion of overall expenditures that will be affected by the handful of key activities over a period of time.

Advantages:

- The hybrid model gives finance executives the tools they are more familiar with.
- It provides a bridge between the "real" financial numbers for expenditures and the estimated net gain realized each time an activity event takes place.
- The process of developing this model often aids in achieving alignment and understanding of the systems under investigation or development.

Disadvantages:

- The presentation of the model's findings must be conceptualized properly for each audience that sees it.
- Most personnel need only see the activity-based findings as it provides a straightforward and compelling case.
- The top-down findings may appear a little weak given the limited scope of the analysis, and it is essential that recipients of these figures understand the context in which they were developed.
- The time required in completing this model can create issues for maintaining project schedules and managing development/consulting costs.

When estimating the ROI for the larger, more complex strategy on the executive level, model B (top-down approach) makes sense: the volume of functional benefits is so large it can no longer be assessed at a granular level. For the smaller and more distinct project phases model A (bottom-up approach) makes sense. Model B is standard teaching material for any MBA and requires financial analytic skills more than an understanding of digital content management. Those financial skills are beyond the scope of this book. It should suffice to mention that the top-down approach is an available method that is often ignored in the marketing-driven space. The remainder of the chapter focuses on Method A, which is directly tied to the tasks and processes of digital content management systems. It is the most common method used in the market space by vendors and analysts alike.

What Is the Role of ROI?

In an ideal case, the ROI is a key component of the business case and delivers valuable data about investment and return. However, ROI calculations, when done correctly, have a role to play beyond the initial business case. They provide the means by which the entire initiative and the individual projects can be measured. The return, expressed in hard numbers or less tangible objectives, should represent the milestones by which the success of each implementation phase is evaluated. By aligning reality to the original target, the estimated investment and returns are project management tools for setting milestones for the budget process and for measuring the degree of success or failure.

As established in the prior chapter, computing investment and return are only part of a larger business case. Establishing a clear vision, defining the exact business problem, and establishing an implementation strategy are equally important elements of the full business case.

The Investment

When establishing the ROI, most calculations focus on the return. The investment is often simplified to software and services costs. That is never the true picture. To begin with, there is a difference in initial or one-time costs and those that will be repeating or ongoing. In addition there are tangible and intangible costs. As with intangible returns, intangible costs are harder to quantify, but they might be significant nonetheless, yet are missing from most ROI calculations. Below we will take a closer look at the different aspects of the required investment.

Initial Costs (Year One)

The following list is a guideline for the costs that need to be considered for the implementation phase, which usually consumes the bigger part of the first year.

External Costs

- License and annual maintenance costs or hosting fees for year one
- Vendor services and customization costs
- Hardware costs
- Consultant costs

Internal Costs (Staff Time)

- Internal project management

- Business analysis (identify and quantify issues)

- Requirements analysis (workflow, use cases, and more)

- Vendor selection

- System configuration

- Migration

- System testing

- Training/Education

- Change management

- Enhancement/Customization definitions

- Staff additions (librarian and potentially management)

- Defining and implementing governance models

As this list shows, the emphasis of these calculations should be on the internal costs. This is contrary to ROI presentations typically seen in the field. For most projects, the internal costs outweigh the external costs by two or three to one. Therefore, mistakes in internal planning and project management usually have a much higher impact on the costs than external mistakes. Poor management of the internal tasks will result in higher numbers for both internal and external costs. Surprising in that regard is that many companies do not employ independent professional help in planning and managing these complex projects.

Calculating Initial Costs

Most calculations for the investment needs are straight-forward. License, maintenance, hardware, and services costs can be obtained from vendors. Consultants should be able to bid their services, and their fees can be tied to success milestones. Internal tasks can be computed by time multiplied with staff costs. The most difficult part of this calculation is establishing a realistic number for internal staff time. Realistic estimates can also be found in similar projects in the vertical industry or from truly unbiased consultants.

When calculating the staff cost, the list in the section above can be a rough guide. Table 7.1 shows an example. For some tasks, staff with significantly different per unit cost should be calculated separately.

TASK	TIME REQUIRED	X	STAFF COST PER TIME UNIT	=	COST OF IMPLEMENTING TASK
Project management	80 days		$400		$32,000
Vendor selection					
Staff	20 days		$400		$8,000
Management	5 days		$800		$4,000
Business analysis					
Staff	100 days		$400		$40,000
Management	10 days		$800		$8,000

TABLE 7.1 *Calculation for Staff Cost of Implementation*

Ongoing Costs

In addition to the initial costs, the system will need to be managed and maintained. As technology constantly changes, upgrades or updates are required, and staff needs to be educated on the new elements and possibilities. At a minimum one should consider the effort required for the following items:

- Administrative overhead
- IT maintenance (database and regular system maintenance)
- Hardware maintenance
- Continued education
- Software maintenance for products
- Software maintenance for customizations
- Upgrades/updates (planning, implementation, testing)
- Expanding/scaling

Calculating Ongoing Costs

Most costs of ongoing operations are also either vendor quotes or staff time. Table 7.2 shows the example of administrative overhead.

ADMIN-ISTRATIVE TASK	TIME (IN HOURS)	X	FRE-QUENCY (MONTHLY)	X	STAFF COST	=	COST PER MONTH
Assigning metadata	.3		150		$50		$2,250
Creating/ editing user accounts	.5		50		$50		$1,250

TABLE 7.2 *Calculating Administrative Overhead*

To establish the additional costs of administration, a matrix like Table 7.2 needs to be prepared for both the situation before and after implementing any changes to processes and/or technology. The administrative tasks should be derived from the business analysis.

In regard to ongoing expenses, it is of particular importance to clarify how potential customizations are updated or upgraded. While most software vendors provide clear agreements on upgrades and updates for standard systems, customizations often lack these definitions. Especially if third parties were involved in building extensions or integrations, it is very important to clarify who is responsible for forward compatibility and how much that will cost. It is normal to incur up to 20% of the development costs as annual maintenance for custom work. However, it is important to clarify that maintenance includes any and all changes necessary to ensure the custom code will work with system upgrades and updates. Make sure to include coding of necessary changes, implementing, and testing. This can be a substantial amount of work requiring also dedicated internal management. If no forward compatibility is guaranteed for custom work, upgrades can add significant time and material costs.

Another aspect to carefully consider in ongoing cost is that of scaling or expansion. Vendors are quick to point to the scaling options of their solutions. However, larger systems often require additional expenditures. As systems become more mission critical, issues such as redundancy, fault tolerance, disaster recovery, and availability become more important and can present significant hardware, IT, and licensing costs. Besides infrastructure, system configuration and taxonomy become much more complex with growing systems, and, therefore, time spent on these internal tasks will increase significantly.

The rule of thumb for expanding systems is that the costs grow exponentially, not linearly. This is true even if the license costs grow linearly or if vendors offer

DEFINED RISK	AFFECTED TASKS	COST	COMMENTS
Schedule Delay	Project management	$400 per day	Resource required
	Migration	$100 per day	Resources in stand by
	Testing	no cost …	…
System outage (bug or technical issue)	All system use	$5,000 day one $15,000 day two and after	Added time for manual completion of tasks

TABLE 7.3 *Calculating Cost Associated with Risk*

deeper discounts with a growing number of users. In general, the total cost of ownership is becoming less tied to licenses with growing systems.

Intangible Costs

As there are intangible returns, there are also intangible costs. Most prominent is "lost productivity." Lost productivity comes in two forms. By diverting staff time to the implementation process, other business processes will receive proportionally less attention as a result. It is hard to calculate the costs stemming from this reallocation of resources, as the costs are not equivalent to the time/cost of staff. However, ignoring the business impact of this reallocation, as most analysts do, creates an unmanaged risk that can be substantial.

The other aspect of productivity loss is represented by the learning curve in regard to the new process and tools. The key question is this: How much time will it take the staff to become proficient with the new processes and practices? As a rule of thumb, add 20% of staff time to the tasks they are required to perform during the ramp up.

Intangible costs are also associated with the project risks. We pointed to one risk above, and the prior chapter addressed building the business case, which includes the analysis of the risks. In some cases these risks have a monetary element. Schedule delays, technical problems, or user adoption issues can increase the costs of a project. Few business cases truly research the risks. Even fewer estimate the cost associated with these risks. This is one reason why projects tend to go over budget. Table 7.3 shows a simplified example to calculate the cost associated with risk. Risk mitigation and back-up planning should be part of the implementation planning and is discussed further in the Chapter 1.

Total Cost of Ownership

It should be obvious that calculating the total cost of ownership (TCO) is a significant effort. Why otherwise highly professional companies trust a quick spreadsheet provided by a vendor's sales team is a good question. The initial implementation costs, the ongoing costs for at least year 2 and 3, intangible costs, and costs associated with identified risks should all be carefully computed and tracked as the implementation progresses. Corrections should be made where necessary, and the new numbers will provide a better base for the estimates of the next implementation phase. Growing competency of one's organization is probably nowhere more important than in the area of estimating and controlling the TCO.

Tangible Return

Tangible returns represent the best measure for the success of a new process or technology, and so are examined in detail in this section. Digital content management projects may have some combination of the following elements come into play.

Savings from Gained Productivity

In general the savings can be calculated by defining the current cost for creating, review and approval, use, reuse, and destruction and then subtracting the future cost of these tasks. The tables 7.4 and 7.5 show an example.

Monthly cost savings for these two tasks: $9,500 - $4,000 = $5,500

Of course this number needs to be compared to the ongoing cost of a potential new solution. Naturally, for these two tasks as defined here, a larger system is no option. However, considering a better organized file structure in the local network might be worth the effort for just these two tasks alone.

The complete list of tasks should be derived from the analysis of the use cases and workflows as described in Chapters 4 and 6. Larger systems should provide many thousands of transactions per month.

TASK	TIME (IN HOURS)	X	FRE- QUENCY (MONTHLY)	X	STAFF COST	=	COST PER MONTH
Locating PowerPoint	.3		300		$50		$4,500
Locating current product description	.2		500		$50		$5,000
Total							$9,500

TABLE 7.4 *Calculating Current Cost*

TASK	TIME (IN HOURS)	X	FRE- QUENCY (MONTHLY)	X	STAFF COST	=	COST PER MONTH
Locating PowerPoint	.1		300		$50		$1,500
Locating current product description	.1		500		$50		$2,500
Total							$4,000

TABLE 7.5 *Calculating Future Cost*

Savings from Expedited Time to Market

Another big gain of Web-based content management systems is the ability to collaborate on review, approval, and localization in near real time.

Most companies have internal calculations about the average cost per day of a product roll out. In that case, the savings of cutting the time to market can then be calculated by simply multiplying the number of days saved with the average costs of roll out per day. Cutting time to market has, of course, other advantages. Many of these additional benefits are more intangible and are discussed below.

New Revenue Opportunities

New revenue usually comes in one or a combination of four forms:

- Transaction

- Subscription

- License

- Advertising

Transaction

E-commerce usually refers to selling goods over the Internet. However, access to libraries of content can also be a revenue source. Agencies might charge a fee to their clients to access the repository of marketing material and the individual files like logos, photos, and graphics. Rather than charging this by credit card as in most consumer e-commence applications, a monthly bill can be prepared with charges for transactions. See Table 7.5 for an example.

TRANSACTION	FEE PER USE	NUMBER OF TRANSACTIONS	TOTAL
Download high-res images	$10	50	$ 500
Download low-res images	$5	250	$1,250
Transformation (to different size or resolution)	$15	100	$1,500
Client Uploads	$20	40	$ 800
Total		440	$4,050

TABLE 7.6 *An Example of Transaction Fee Tabulation*

Subscription

A subscription fee is a fixed fee for a certain time period. Often the fee is based on the size of the system in terms of number of users (named or concurrent) as well as the overall storage availability. Most hosted systems employ this kind of revenue model.

For example: A $3,000 monthly fee allow 20 concurrent users and 10 GB of storage with unlimited transactions.

However, creativity has all the options here. A system might allow a fixed number of transactions for a base subscription fee and then charge for transactions beyond that number (cell phone model).

License

A license agreement is most often used for systems that are installed at a client's site. Licenses are in most cases limited to the number of named users (or seats) or concurrent users.

Advertising

In addition, new revenue sources might be found in advertisement income from new digital distribution channels such as the Web, public display screens (i.e., at airports or retailers), or personal handheld devices.

Business models that aim for new revenue sources are a central theme in many transition and change strategies for companies today. The vision of a future state in which digital content is repurposed and delivered through new channels and in new forms and formats is often a motivating factor to engage in a larger digital strategy. Key words are: one-to-one marketing, on-demand, interactive, targeted. It should be stressed, however, that the changes required to transform an organization into a digital enterprise are no small undertaking. This small section about the basic models should be weighed against the bigger issues of building the business case and the required change management, as discussed in Chapter 6 and Chapter 2, respectively.

Saving in Shipping and Handling Costs

Another often significant source of return is in saved shipping costs. Many review and approval processes can be accomplished digitally over the Web. These processes can involve dozens of users and multiple iterations of files. Shipping and handling costs for just one marketing brochure can reach thousands of dollars. In many cases the Web-based processes can eliminate shipping of CDs or tapes entirely.

Intangible Return

Intangible returns are harder to calculate, but many digital content management systems are implemented primarily for the intangible gain. Below, the common intangible gains are described in detail.

Brand Compliance

Companies worldwide have come to realize that brands are often their most valuable asset. Management of that brand or brands, the image, message, and geographical nuances is complex and resource intensive. Digital content management systems, in particular rich media management systems, can greatly improve an organization's control over its branding. By providing centrally controlled access to brand elements like current logos, images, and approved marketing material, creators of branding content are much less likely to be off message or to use outdated elements. Global review and approval via the Web can be efficient and fairly easy.

Legal Compliance (Less Litigation)

Legal compliance does not just include compliance with regulatory guidelines, but also covers areas of copyright or other agreements that govern the right to use or distribute content or elements of content. Infringing on these rights can be very costly. The technologies available to rights owners become more effective to track misse via the Web (see Chapter 5 on DRM). While the most prominent examples of enforcement of rights in the digital age focused on a few teenagers being sued by the music conglomerates, the issue for any organization is not much different. One goal of digital content management can be to ensure better control over content that is governed by limiting usage or copyright agreements.

Improved Communications

There are various processes and workflows that can be enhanced with online content management tools. Even without fully automating every aspect, a content management system can, for example, allow a client to view in real time the images, videos, or other content that has been uploaded. Comments and decisions can be tracked as metadata, and reports can create great clarity about communication. Who made a comment and when? Who approved?

Sending a press kit to thousands of journalists is now a job of a few mouse clicks. The kit arrives via a branded e-mail message. Last minute changes can be accomplished in seconds.

Improved Competitive Position

As mentioned above in the section about time to market, competitive positioning can be a key business rational for driving efficiency-enhancing initiatives.

Competitors in the case of time to market are not only comparable products or services from other vendors, but also the black market and illegal duplication that has become a huge competitive issue in some industries. Nowadays fake DVDs are available within days of major film releases. To keep that share of revenue, movie studios have to finetune their creation and delivery operations to extreme standards. The required level of efficiency is simply not possible without digital workflows.

Competitive positioning can also mean that an organization is either leading or following the trend of new service offerings. In some cases, these services are created as loss leaders intended to bind clients closer to the organization thus the calculated loss should be less than the cost of new client acquisitions via traditional means. An example can be the printer who makes all printed material available for review online. Allowing the client to browse and search for print material will please the print buyer, who can now find out exactly what material the printer has or is missing. Moreover, a well-designed solution has the potential of extending the reach of the printer beyond the print buyer into the client's organization by providing a quick reference to marketing teams or other groups with high printing needs, as well. Creating extended service offerings like this not only binds the client to the vendor, but it also opens new business opportunities.

Improved Staff Awareness of Company IP

By providing tools and processes that allow easier access (i.e., Web browser) and more intuitive search interfaces for finding the crucial IP of an organization, it is likely that the staff is becoming more aware of the available information. In fact they might be able to browse for information on the sole assumption that something might exist. This is specifically true for information that might be not part of the immediate day-to-day tasks. For example: an automobile manufacturer might provide all training videos and related material in an easily searchable, complete archive. That allows the engine group to find and review the production process of the assembly team in matter of minutes. In turn this can impact the design of the next generation engine.

Increased Number of Use and Reuse of IP

If intuitive systems, combined with training and change management, are allowing users to find information in minutes that used to take days to pin down, they most likely start reusing content that they would not have used prior, due to the ease of finding what they need. This cuts down on the significant cost of reproducing existing material over and over again.

Summary

There are different models for calculating ROI. Independent of the models used ROI calculations provide important data not only for the initial financial planning and the business case. The numbers are an important project management tool in that they are setting clear targets. However, calculating the complex and often disruptive innovation that a large digital content management system represents is difficult and requires specific knowledge about the workflows and tasks affected by the new tools and processes.

In addition, intangible costs and returns are often significant elements of the business case. Therefore a well built ROI is a project in itself. It will take significant effort and should be staffed with experienced resources.

8 Expanding the System Hardware and Software

This chapter addresses issues related to hardware and software when moving from single or point solutions to a services platform for digital media management on an enterprise scale. As this book is not deeply technical, certain concepts will be simplified to some degree. The goal is to raise awareness of some larger issues related to the planning and implementation of a larger strategy. One application does not necessarily have to contain all of the desired functionalities. A content management system might consist of different "smart" applications working together. To understand the issues, it is necessary to understand at least on a high level what a content management system does. Chapter 3 described the core elements and the peripheral tools on a very high level. Following is a closer definition.

Business Logic

The core of a content management system is its business logic: the rules that govern who sees what, when, and how to find assets. As simple as it sounds, this is a highly complicated system that requires years of expertise to be built well, especially if the number of transactions reaches into the thousands or tens of thousands per day. It therefore is common and acceptable that the core logic is a proprietary system.

Many vendors offer some degree of business process automation as an integrated package with their solution. Systems, which define rules and routes, are an entirely separate set of applications than those that manage a repository, with its metadata and security schema. In most cases there will be different databases and potentially even a separate storage location for assets "in transit." There is nothing wrong with vendors that offer both as one package as long as the functionality will meet requirements now and in the future.

> The flexibility and openness of the architecture will become more and more important as any enterprise system and its requirements grow and diversify. The questions to consider are: How separated are the different components in the system? What degree of scalability do the different elements offer, and what happens if changes are made?

On a high level, in addition to the core application, the different elements to consider are:

- The tools for data preparation and manipulation as defined in Chapter 3 (i.e., scanning and optical character recognition, image transformations, indexing, and more)

- A system to present files and data in the user interface (browser-based in the best case)

- A database to manage the metadata relationships, user information, and more

- A storage system to store files and data

- Integration or communication bridges to other creative or business applications (i.e., plug in to a creative desktop application like Photoshop, integration with business process automation systems, or communication with accounting systems)

These and other peripheral elements, while in themselves potentially proprietary systems, should be tied to the core application in an open standards-based fashion. In basic terms: if the average programmer cannot exchange one media processing engine with another without touching proprietary code, he will be forced to use the services of vendors each time he makes a change. The same is true for the user interface and storage solution. If these elements of the system are not open, the vendor's potentially expensive services must be used, and the system will most likely be restricted in implementation and system design.

Design Considerations for a Growing System

Design decisions will become more important as the system grows. For example, there is now a variety of free open source products available with more to come that might easily fulfill the system's requirements (Apache Web Server and Image Magic, to name two). No matter what the preference of vendor might be, it is important to have a number of choices.

In systems that handle only a limited number of use cases, the general system architecture might be less important. Outsourced systems that host the entire application and infrastructure are a very good alternative for a point solution.

In the case of clean scaling in size, one will have to consider that users and administrators have much more to look at now. It will become more important and more complex to represent the administration functions intuitively and to potentially have multiple dedicated administration interfaces for different levels of administrators. The inflexibility of the UI is often the first limitation of a closed system. Therefore, the degree of separation is especially important for the interface or presentation layer. The end of the chapter discusses the interface considerations.

When considering a shift from silo digital content management solutions to digital media management as a services platform for the enterprise, it is crucial to focus on the flexibility and openness of the system and all its components. As all vendors of larger systems will promise exactly that, it can be confusing to define what truly constitutes an open system. It should be noted that open, flexible, and adaptable are actually three different requirements, but they are most often seen as one, and "open" stands for all three aspects. Following is a description of open systems.

There are three elements that make a system more or less open and therefore more or less flexible and adaptable:

- The general architecture

- The availability, implementation, and documentation of APIs

- The software capabilities and limitations

General Architecture

There are two concepts that are most relevant to the general architecture: Services Oriented Architecture (SOA) and the n-tier back end architecture. SOA implies that the elements that make up the system (the core elements as well as all tools and

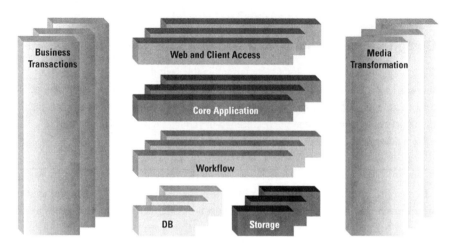

FIGURE 8.1 *The n-tier Architecture*

peripheral elements) are viewed as somewhat independent service providers. They can be called upon by different processes depending on the need. Think of it as departments: the legal team, the sales team, and the marketing team. The teams make up the system, but they can be called upon by anybody inside or outside of the system to do a job for which they have been created.

These elements are usually built on an n-tier infrastructure that includes one or multiple application servers, databases, file systems, and dedicated special service servers, like an image transformation server.

The key advantage of the n-tier architecture is that the different elements are clearly distinguished, illustrated in Figure 8.1. This enables scaling of only those elements where one needs more. If a big load on text indexing is expected, for example, then that element can be built into a distributed service environment (multiple servers in potentially different locations) to ensure high capacity and fault tolerance. Moreover, if the tool currently in use is not sufficient for this use (or the opposite, too advanced and expensive), this architecture makes it easier to replace it.

There is more to it, however, than just separating the tools and elements. A big question is how they communicate with each other and what happens to that communication if changes are made. This leads to the second concept of open systems, the communication between the different parts.

The Availability, Implementation, and Documentation of APIs

Just as there are specific rules and processes that need to be followed when requesting services from a legal or marketing team, the different elements of each system will follow certain rules and processes to communicate. The communication between the elements of the system is defined in a set of application program interfaces or APIs.

The protocols and standards available for this kind of communication are examined in the next chapter. In brief, this communication can become a key element in the scaling process for the system. If thousands of requests, confirmations, and notifications need to be communicated between servers, then a sophisticated traffic system is required. An open system will distinguish itself in this area by using well-known standards and protocols and a very well documented system of requests and fulfillment, often managed with what is called request brokers.

It also needs to be very clear what kind of services can be requested and how to do so. To use the team example again, imagine a translation team that translates certain documents. To begin with, is there such a team? If the company has not documented it anywhere, how would anyone know? What kind of information will this team need in order to do its job (source language, target language, target audience, types of documents, and such)? Therefore, good documentation for an open SOA will include a listing of all services and the related APIs that a system provides, how to request those services (how to call the APIs), and what information the system needs to fulfill the services.

If these processes are well-defined and described, there is a much better chance of adjusting and expanding the system to the company's needs. For example, if the company needs a translation into a language the system does not provide, the protocols can be used to request the services of another service provider which might or might not be part of the local system. One might need to add features or functionality to the system beyond the original plan or beyond the feature set a chosen vendor provides out-of-the-box. In that case it is not only the availability and documentation of the application interfaces that will be important, but it will also be the way that they are implemented.

It is almost impossible to test the implementation of these APIs without having concrete examples or use cases. But there is a big difference in the implementation of APIs for use with existing functionality only and those that are specifically designed to interface with elements and system that were not defined at the time the interface was designed. In the translation example, it could be that the protocols allow for two byte characters (Japanese, Chinese, and Korean, for example), although the feature set of the application does not include that capability out-of-the-box. A well-designed system anticipates the need for change. That is true for the capabilities in terms of communication interfaces, but is also true for the design of the software itself.

The Software Capabilities and Limitations

Last but not least in the line of important factors concerning the open nature of a solution is the software that drives the core applications. Similar to the APIs, the key question is if the software was written for a specific use case or if it was intentionally designed to be flexible. In the area of digital content management, taxonomies play an important part (see Chapter 10 for more detail). Therefore, the functionality and flexibility of the software tools in regard to building, representing, and maintaining taxonomies is a good example for this principal: how many parallel structures can be built; can they be hierarchical; do they inherit up or down the tree; can they include synonyms and misspellings; can they be controlled lists; can they be multilingual; can they reference other external taxonomies; can the maintenance be broken down into sub-sections; and so on.

Today, few systems have been designed from the outset as platforms for SOA. Most systems were closed to begin with and had a narrow application focus. As the market demanded more open systems, parts of the code were rewritten, and API layers were added to satisfy the most common requirements. At a minimum, this allows vendors to add the buzz words to their brochures. The marketing material is not a good guide for evaluating the robustness and maturity of technology in terms of extensibility and flexibility. Engineering expertise and concrete use cases are required to truly evaluate the degree of openness.

However, there are other more obvious aspects that will determine the usefulness of technology in a larger digital content management platform. Following is a look at the specific elements that make up the system, and what issues may arise out of expanding the system. The next chapter will focus on issues related to integration, so that topic is not detailed here.

Core Application

The first question to ask about the core application is this: does the system need an application built to support one or a limited number of use cases or "solutions" or does it need to create a services oriented platform built on a high capacity back end application which can be used in various solutions depending on the integration with other tools and a flexible UI framework? The answer might be both.

It may start by expanding or adding a few specific use cases, but eventually the goal may be to build more integrated or interconnected systems.

There are a few important concepts for scaling the core application, but it is important to keep the big picture in mind. If a point solution can create significant return on investment (ROI) in a short time frame, there is nothing wrong with implementing it even if it will be redundant later on. Specifically, a hosted solution with limited capital expenditures can be a useful interim tool.

If the enterprise platform approach is pursued, then it is advisable to consider the following in regards to the core digital content management application:

Vendor Company

In addition to the obvious financial health of the vendor, the road map for the application(s) should be is aligned with the goals of the project. Mergers and acquisitions of small and midsize technology companies can have an effect on the road map.

The importance of API documentation has been described above. In that respect it is also important to clarify the maturity of the support organizations. Will the project team have access to development level support from the vendor and at what cost?

Last, a general vendor reference should come from the preferred integration partners. Who has built solutions on top of the application framework to be purchased and what has been their experience? Are these independent service providers available for new work?

Pricing

When it comes to pricing, there are usually two options. Seat and concurrent user models calculate the software license fee based on the number of users that the system will serve. CPU-based pricing models calculate the fees on the capacity of the system, independent of human interaction. In many cases, these models can be applied in combination.

The concurrent license model charges for concurrent connections, independent of the total number of users who access the system in a given period. The seat model charges by named users, independent of how many users use the system at the same time, how often they will do so, or how long they will use the system on average. The concurrent user model is the more flexible model, but it requires some calculations of the expected concurrent usage. An advantage is that the license can always be expanded to include more connections. If this becomes necessary, it is for good reason — the system is being used.

But all pricing models based on human users have limits, especially in an SOA. Requests for services of the application might come from other applications rather than humans. For example, an application might request data associated with a certain unique ID. This could be in combination with a request from a separate system that confirms the authentication of content or from a digital rights management application (DRM). These requests can often be handheld in milliseconds and are therefore very different from a human user that requires more resource intensive transactions. In this case, the CPU pricing model is more suitable. The CPU model is sometimes also called server pricing. In both cases the idea is that a defined level of computing performance will result in a defined fee (i.e., $50k per Intel® Xeon™ Processor or comparable performing CPU).

Regardless of pricing model, volume discounts should allow to pay less as one buys more. For very large systems, vendors often offer enterprise licenses that allow unlimited scaling within the enterprise. In those cases, only the maintenance fees increase as the system is rolled out.

As was mentioned in the prior chapters about the business case, it is a general rule in larger systems that licenses fees are becoming a decreasing part of the total cost of owner ship as systems grow. Integration, customization, training, and other internal costs are climbing, while license fees will be usually discounted as their use grows.

Performance

Naturally, performance is an important element in determining the viability of a product for large-scale issues. Vendors provide performance metrics that define how their application behaves under load. However, this data depends on many variants (network, file size, number of simultaneous requests, complexity of requests, and so on). In addition to the vendor's matrix, the number of instances for the key processes that are recommended should be checked and compared to any limitation of the license. An instance is comparable to the number of open cash registers at a supermarket. The load distribution between the instances is hopefully a bit more sophisticated, but the idea is the same. Requests are spread across the available instances and processed in order.

Depending on the design of the application, one instance may be able to handle more than one request in parallel. That ability is called multithreading. It allows the server to provide parallel feedback to multiple tasks rather than queuing them up. A queue can potentially mean longer response times for everybody if a specific task takes a long time. It is similar to waiting for someone to write a check at the supermarket. In a multithreaded world that cashier would start the next customer's check-out while the other person can take plenty of time writing the check.

Technical expertise is required to truly evaluate this advantage, but it is fair to assume that in most cases a multithreading application will handle load better than a single threading one. However, multithreading is significantly more complex to program and it requires highly skilled developers. Some elements of the system might simply not be available as a multithreaded application. The ability to perform asynchronous processes is important, especially if the application of choice is single threaded.. Asynchronous processes are usually those that take a long time (i.e., download of a high resolution file or a complex transformation from one file type to another). In that case, it is important that a user will not have to wait until that process is finished before performing other actions. A large download request can run asynchronously and send a notification when it is done, via e-mail for example. A user can then access the file at a local staging area. Think of dry cleaning. One drops it off and picks it up when it is done. There is no need to wait in the store.

Open Source

In addition to applications from proprietary vendors, consider open source applications like Plone (http://plone.org/) built on Zope (http://www.zope.org/), which is currently the most complete solution. For a list of additional open source systems, see the OS CMS Directory in the resources section.

Pricing of open source systems is simpler. Users typically pay nothing for the software but then most likely need specialized services to build the system. These services will be available at similar rates than services from proprietary vendors. However, users will also have to pay for regular maintenance and support of open source software. The rates for that service can be higher than the annual maintenance of proprietary software. Total cost of ownership for open source systems might not be significantly lower, which is contrary to what "free software" might suggest. The real advantage of open source systems is that they are open, as defined above. The downside is that managing the implementation without vendor-prepared documentation and help is difficult. Open source is written by community contributors and not for the average IT guy. Often, newer versions of open source products will not consider backward compatibility issues as the community strives for the best implementation of a technology, not for an easy upgrade path. Proprietary vendors are usually more considerate of that issue.

Open source is therefore a good solution for technically savvy and skilled companies that have significant capability to ensure that the support and implementation of open source products is not an uncontrolled risk. Educational institutions like universities and schools are an example. However, there are service companies that focus on delivering turnkey solutions built on open source. In the area of content management, various commercial projects have used open source with much success. See the resources section for more information.

The Peripheral Tools

When it comes to peripheral tools, the level of integration can vary widely.

The areas of peripheral tools include

- **Desktop Application Plug-Ins**
  e.g., Seamless check-in and check-out to the repository from creative tools such as QuarkXPress, Adobe Creative Suite, Dreamweaver, or text-based editing tools such as MS Word.

- **Server-based media preparation, transformation, and indexing tools**
  e.g., Image transformation (resizing, file type conversions), parsing of metadata from essence, text indexing for text search databases, and more.

For larger systems the key question is how the communication and integration between the core application and these tools is accomplished. As mentioned above, functionality and flexibility in the implementation are two different things. In an open system demons and request brokers are designed to handle the communication between the tools and the core application. If they are built to scale in any direction and include well-documented APIs, the services can be added and scaled when needed.

The priority for vendors in this highly competitive market is often the need to announce a certain functionality or feature. The quality and flexibility of the underlying integration is not always as important. Pre-packaged solutions might offer functionality quickly, but this advantage has to be carefully weighed against needed flexibility down the road. This topic is continued in the next chapter.

Database

As with all elements of the system, the database should be an open and standards-based product. It should be highly optimizable, and ideally the optimizations can follow the database vendor's directions without limitation by the core content management application. Databases offer many possible integration points, although in complex content management environments, it is usually recommended to read the data and not to write. This is due to the business logic that is built into the application. While it might be possible to add a value or row to the database directly, this might circumvent elements of the business logic such as security and reporting of transactions.

Databases are primarily a tool for searching the content and for data mining and reporting. They provide information to users, administrators, and other systems such as what file is where, who accessed it and when, how many users are using the system, what are they looking for, and so on.

An important question for larger systems is the option for federated searches across multiple databases potentially distributed across different locations. A company might have multiple digital content management systems that each has a unique ability for a segment of the business. Rather than forcing the same system on all users, it may make sense to let users use the system that works for them and also create a unified view into the repositories with federated search options. This is true for multiple internal systems and also for external systems.

An example that integrates an external system could be an image library that is both an internal repository of images and also tied to a stock photography house. Users might search by keywords for "Young Couple Golden Gate Bridge." This search can produce the internal hits and indicate them as such as well as those images found at the stock photography house in one seamless interface. While the process to download or receive the images might be different, this ability to search multiple data stores in one action can save time and foster reuse practices.

Storage/Archiving

The current system might have built-in archiving options, but it is good to understand what actually happens with archived content. In general, there are the following three options:

- **Online:** The content stays online but it is "hidden" from end users. Archiving is simply a status change or tag in the system.

- **Near-line:** The content might move to a dedicated location such as a tape or optical disk (more likely in systems that manage massive amounts of data or native files, because these files are much larger than structured data). Near-line storage usually keeps content available via the usual interface, but it might affect the time it takes to access the content.

- **Off-line:** Content can be archived off-line on CDs, DVDs, drives, or tapes that are stored in physical archives, possibly in separate locations. In this case, a well-designed system should have the option to keep low-resolution proxies or summaries of the content available for search and potentially provide an option to order high-resolution files or full versions.

Any larger vendor that provides storage solutions will usually offer also storage management software. Hierarchical storage management (HSM) is what the largest content system will require to fully automate the process.

Distributed Storage

It is not always feasible to store all content in one location. This is specifically the case if the content consists of large files like high-res video or large high-res images. During the creation or editing process, these files need to be accessed frequently, and it can be difficult to accommodate the users if the files have to be pulled from remote servers. Bandwidth limitations can create unacceptable wait times, and the likelihood of file corruptions increases with very large file transfers. Under these circumstances, the core application should be able to control multiple file stores across the network. There are different mechanisms that can allow that control. If a company has very large files or other reasons for needing multiple storage locations, it should make sure to evaluate the application's ability to manage a distributed storage environment.

Network

In regards to the network there are two main points to consider: speed and security.

Network Speed or Bandwidth

With gigabit networks now becoming affordable, internal bandwidth is not a big issue, in most cases. However, large digital content management systems often span multiple locations or even require external access by contractors, partners, or customers/consumers. In those cases network bandwidth can become an issue.

There are multiple ways to control the network requirements regarding speed/bandwidth. One is to look to the file and ensure users are in fact accessing files in a format required for their work. Files with lower resolution or smaller size may be sufficient to accomplish the required tasks. The content management strategy should include the creation and management of proxies in lower file sizes than the original. Another possibility is to control the way that large files are delivered. The possibility of asynchronous processes — such as scheduling delivery of larger files — was discussed earlier in this chapter in the section "Performance."

Another option is to look at the network itself and ensure optimal utilization. Multiple Protocol Label Switching (MPLS) is a relatively new option to increase network efficiency. But there are other aspects, such as edge servers and point-to-point networks, that allow delivery of large files in acceptable timeframes. Edge technology refers to a system of storing a certain part of large files (usually streaming video) on a distributed network of servers. If a user requests a file, the stored portion will stream from the nearest server, while the rest of the file is then requested from the original store. This is similar to the buffering users may notice when accessing streaming media from a web browser. The buffer is what is stored on the various servers which are in this in case referred to as edge servers.

A point-to-point network is self-explanatory. The issue here is cost. It is more expensive to build a dedicated connection between two or multiple locations than it is to use the public Internet. However, compared with shipping costs for DVDs or tapes, the cost for a point-to-point network might be feasible.

Network Security

Issues related to this topic were discussed in Chapter 4. Here it should suffice that encryption (SSL) and virtual private networks (VPN) provide a high level of security for relatively low cost. Every IT team should have knowledge of these technologies.

Desktop Clients and UIs

Maybe the most important technology requirement in a larger system is the ability to build independent and integrated interfaces easily. Ideally, a system has tools for building UIs and modular elements that can be combined in any fashion and can also be incorporated into the templates of another system.

There are three kinds of interfaces to most digital content applications. The modern UI is most commonly a browser-based thin client that does not require installation of software on the user's computer. These thin clients should support at least Microsoft's Internet Explorer for the PC and Safari for the Mac and maybe Firefox for either platform.

However, certain workflows that involve creative tools like the Adobe Creative Suite, Apple's Final Cut Pro, or other content creation tools require integration with these well-established application interfaces. There are multiple approaches to integrations of that kind. The goal is that key functionality like check-in and check-out or even basic services can be performed right from the creative application. The user is not required to change to a different application. We will discuss this topic further in the next chapter.

A third kind of interface is known as the thick client. These are applications that need to be installed on a user's computer to support specific functionality. Thick clients are often used for application administration interfaces and also for functionality that integrates operating system tools like drag and drop.

To fully evaluate the flexibility and expandability of an application, one will have to look into the specifics for the creation of all three kinds of interfaces. A truly open application will have defined tools and APIs to build or customize all three types of UI.

Summary

It is the flexibility of the system architecture that sets the true enterprise players apart from the departmental systems that may boast of additional features and functionality. When planning a system expansion, one should keep in mind that a monolithic stand-alone application will harbor many limitations in comparison to an open, integrated solution that is designed to communicate with the existing IT infrastructure. However, the latter requires more technical understanding and planning. The implementation might be more complex. One option is to expand with very focused solutions, specifically in the first implementation phases. Those solutions can even be hosted by vendors, which can eliminate or significantly reduce IT expenditures.

In a larger, horizontally expanding system, it is crucial to carefully consider how flexible and open the system needs to be to allow an expansion in any direction necessary.

9 Integration

Digital content management systems in themselves represent a significant value for any business or organization by streamlining creation, management, and distribution of digital content and information. However, an even larger value lies in combining that control of the content with other business functions. For media and entertainment companies — where digital content represents the core business asset — tying these assets to other business processes is essential. The digital content management strategy of the digital media enterprise should aim at an integrated end-to-end digital backbone consisting of:

- Digital content production

- Digital content management

- Digital rights management

- Licenses/agreements management (B2B)

- Use and user data aggregation (CRM)

- Financial transaction and subscription management

- Supply chain management

These functions will have different priorities for different organizations and can be serviced by a variety of proprietary or open source systems. Some systems might be dedicated to a specific use case while others are utilized in a number of use cases. Ideally the complexity of the information flow between the systems is transparent to the users. Both internal and external users are served with targeted interfaces that provide access to content as well as information about the content in the form and format required via intuitive search, display, and reporting interfaces as well as digital delivery channels.

To accomplish this goal, flexibility and open systems are required, as discussed in Chapter 8. This chapter tries to take a view of the requirements for interconnecting these systems in an enterprise architecture or enterprise services platform. There are various protocols, program environments, and program languages that are common in the space.

Enterprise Architecture

Figure 9.1 shows the breakdown of the key elements in enterprise architecture. There are four different functions or layers in any digital media enterprise system, representing the various uses and features of the system.

The Presentation Layer provides the function of presenting information and/or files to users of the system. Traditional analog presentation and physical media delivery in the form of print, CD/DVD, or broadcast can be viewed as part of that layer, although physical production of these media types might fall outside of the IT architecture. However, much of the production process even for traditionally delivered media can be automated and should be tied to the core services. (i.e., computer to plate printing, made-to-order DVD production, and more)

The Application Services, Middleware, or Framework Layer illustrates the various applications that provide support for certain business functions. These applications communicate requests to and from the core business layer, but they are very targeted and therefore not part of the core services. This layer may also provide pre-packaged communication services. (i.e., e-commerce, map mashing, or workflow) A framework of functional elements will enable the quick building of targeted user interfaces. For example, the framework might provide hooks for certain core services functionality like search for content by keywords.

The Core Services Layer shows those services that feed information and content to the functions higher in the stack. These core functions might also communicate with each other but usually at a request of a user or application higher in the stack For example, an internal account manager of a newspaper might want to see the invoiced amounts alongside a visual representation of the ads that were placed by a specific customer Information from the accounting, customer and digital asset management systems are combined to create the view.

Presentation	Browser-Based UIs	Thick Clients	Creator Application Plugins	Print/CD/DVD/ Tape/ Broadcast
Application Services Framework or Middleware	Java, NET, or Soap/ XML APIs	Proprietary Toolkits, Frameworks and APIs	Perl, Python, NET or Java Applications (i.e, e-commerce Workflow)	
	Digital Asset Management	Financial Accounting and Transaction Management	Supply Chain Management	
Core Services	Digital Rights Management	Subscription and Customer Relationship Management	WebContent Management	
Data and File Store	Databases	User Authentication	File Stores	

FIGURE 9.1 *Simplified View of an Enterprise Architecture*

The Data Layer represents the raw data and files like photos, video, text, PowerPoint presentations, and such. This data is generally not stored in just one location, for security and redundancy. The prior chapter dealt with specific hardware issues of this layer. The most basic user information is stored in this data layer as well.

Integrating Creative and Editorial Tools

The ideal work environment for the creative and editorial staff is usually the creative or editorial application and not the content management application. The creative applications, such as Adobe Creative Suite, QuarkXPress, Avid or Final Cut Pro, provide very specific and very complex functionality. In addition, very targeted scheduling and text-based editing tools such as ENPS (Electronic News Production System for TV News) or QPS (Quark Production System for newspapers) are common in the complex workflows of digital media generation.

The digital content management system cannot replace these refined tools. At the same time, new inefficiencies are introduced if creative and editorial staffs are asked to manage two different systems: their tools set and the digital content management tools. The best solution is to integrate the key content management elements with the creative tools, so that the creative tools become part of the presentation and application services layer of the enterprise architecture. It should, for example, be possible for a photo editor to check-in and check-out an image from the DAM system with the File commands in the photo editing software. In effect, he or she would never leave their preferred work environment while benefiting from the robust content management system.

The vendors of the creative and editorial tools have realized that need. To be classified as an enterprise-ready software tool, vendors have made it easier for these integrations to occur. For text-editing tools such as those used for newspaper or Web site production, the import and export of text in standardized marked up format is becoming common (mostly XML based). For example, Microsoft announced in the summer of 2005 that its new version of MS Office will save documents by default as XML. This simplifies the integration and communication between the core services, such as the digital archive and the higher layers of the stack such as text editing tools.

On the other hand, it must be pointed out that the emerging new standards are not yet fully matured and that the processes of utilizing them are in its infancy. While integrations between systems have become easier, it is still a significant effort to tie multiple systems together. XML alone is no guarantor for harmonized data models and information flow. Most vendors develop their own flavor of XML. In order to find content in a large archive and to find the crucial information about that content, such as usage rights or content owner, the information must be harmonized and carefully organized. The issue of classification systems and metadata models will be discussed in Chapters 10 and 11.

To harmonize different flavors of XML and other integration technologies, a simple rule can be followed. The less proprietary the flavor and the more open the system, the easier it will be to mold the information flow into the required form and format. Open systems were discussed in Chapter 8.

Integrating Different CM Systems

Integration of different digital content management systems is another important element of a successful enterprise strategy. For example it might be necessary to integrate a rich media repository of a DAM system with an existing CMS. In that case it should be possible to do so by utilizing well-documented and field-proven application program interfaces (APIs). Simple Object Access Protocol (SOAP) and/or Java Remote Method Invocation (RMI) APIs are common.

A good and publicly available example of a well implemented integration between DAM and CMS is the Multimedia Gallery on DuPont's public Web site at http://online-pressroom.net/dupont/. The upper navigation frame contains the makings of a CMS, while the lower frame provides access to the repository via an intuitive search interface. These relatively easy integrations are the key in building integrated solutions and systems for the enterprise.

Integrating Business Processes

As in the prior examples in this chapter, integration between core business processes is best accomplished via APIs. Of specific interest in this case is the fact that vendors of core business systems, such as financial or customer relationship management systems, are faced with a specific problem. While they manage the most valuable assets and information, they are also the most hidden from the user. They are often referred to as back end or back office applications. That presents problems for sales and marketing because the traditional idea of buying a software product usually meant that a potential customer could see an interface that allows for demonstration of certain use cases or functionality.

Vendors in this space have to bridge the concept of requiring a "head-less" engine with maximum flexibility, scalability, and integration options with the need to demonstrate what they actually do. One successful approach for these vendors has been to demonstrate solutions — instances of user interfaces that accomplished certain tasks or use cases. Examples could be the compliance solutions that almost every digital content management vendor offers today.

The problem with this in regards to an enterprise integration strategy is that a well-defined solution for a specific problem says very little about the flexibility, scalability, and integration options of the application. Think of it as a car. If the requirement asks for a specific car model, the engine is not necessarily the key concern as long as it meets the specific need for this particular car. But if the requirement is an engine for use in various models and for various purposes, the focus should be on the engine not on the nice leather interior or other features of a specific model. Therefore it is very important to distinguish between the core services and other applications that are higher in the stack and fulfill more targeted services.

Clarification of Concepts and Terms

Architectural Concepts and Terms

SOA – Services Oriented Architecture

The term Service Oriented Architecture (SOA) expresses a software architectural concept that defines the use of services to support the requirements of software users. In a SOA environment, nodes on a network make resources available to other participants in the network as independent services that the participants access in a standardized way. Most definitions of SOA identify the use of Web services (using SOAP and WSDL) in its implementation. However, one can implement SOA using any service-based technology.

Unlike traditional object-oriented architectures, SOAs comprise loosely joined, highly interoperable application services. Because these services interoperate over different development technologies (such as Java and .NET), the software components become very reusable.

SOA provides a methodology and framework for documenting enterprise capabilities and can support integration and consolidation activities.

SOA is not a product, although several vendors offer products which can form the basis of a SOA. Examples of such products include (alphabetical by vendor):

* BEA Systems: WebLogic Platform & AquaLogic
* Cordys: Business Collaboration Platform
* General Dynamics: Openwings
* Microsoft: Indigo Application Server
* IBM: WebSphere Platform
* SAP: Netweaver
* Sun Microsystems: Java Enterprise System
* TIBCO Software: BusinessWorks & Service Deployment Platform (Project Matrix)

High-level languages such as BPEL or WS-coordination take the service concept one step further by providing a method of defining and supporting workflows and business processes.

API – Application Program Interface and SDK – Software Development Kit

An application programming interface (API) is a set of definitions of the ways one piece of computer software communicates with another. It is a method of achieving abstraction, usually (but not necessarily) between lower-level and higher-level software. One of the primary purposes of an API is to provide a set of commonly-used functions — for example, to draw windows or icons on the screen. Programmers can then take advantage of the API by incorporating its functionality into their own work, saving them the task of programming everything from scratch. APIs are abstract: software that provides a certain API is often called the implementation of that API. In many instances, an API is synonymous with a software development kit (SDK). An SDK may include an API as well as other tools/hardware, so the two terms are not strictly interchangeable.

Programming Environments and Languages
Microsoft.NET

The .NET framework created by Microsoft is a software development platform focused on rapid application development (RAD), platform independence and network transparency. .NET is Microsoft's strategic initiative for server and desktop development for the next decade. According to Microsoft, .NET includes many technologies that are designed to facilitate rapid development of Internet and intranet applications.

.NET has brought new functionalities and tools to the application programming interface (API). These innovations allow programmers to develop applications for both Windows and the Web as well as components and services (Web services). .NET provides a new reflective, object-oriented API. .NET is designed to be sufficiently generic that many different high-level languages can be compiled.

The .NET framework is a competing product to Sun's Java Virtual Machine (JVM) technology and from there it copies many concepts.

There is a collection of development tools specifically developed for use with the .NET platform. The principal example is Visual Studio .NET, an integrated development environment from Microsoft.

Java 2 Platform Enterprise Edition (a.k.a. Java EE)

Java 2 Platform, Enterprise Edition or Java EE is a programming platform for developing and running distributed multi-tier architecture applications, based largely on modular components running on an application server. The Java EE platform is defined by a specification. Java EE is also considered informally to be a language or standard because providers must agree to certain conformance requirements in order to declare their products as Java EE compliant; albeit with no ISO or ECMA standard.

Java EE includes several API specifications, for example JDBC, client-side applets, RPC, CORBA, and defines how to coordinate them. Java EE features some specifications unique to Java EE for components. These include Enterprise Java Beans, Servlets, Java Server Pages and several Web Services technologies. This allows the developer to create an enterprise application that is portable between platforms and scalable, while integrating with several legacy technologies.

Perl, Python, and Others

Perl is a general-purpose programming language originally developed for text manipulation and now used for a wide range of tasks including system administration, Web development, network programming, graphical user interface (GUI) development, and more.

The language is intended to be practical (easy to use, efficient, complete) rather than beautiful (tiny, elegant, minimal). Its major features are that it is easy to use, supports both procedural and object-oriented (OO) programming, has powerful built-in support for text processing, and has one of the world's most impressive collections of third-party modules.

Python is an interpreted, interactive programming language created by Guido van Rossum in 1990. Python is fully dynamically typed and uses automatic memory management; it is thus similar to Perl. Python is developed as an open source project, managed by the non-profit Python Software Foundation. Python 2.4.1 was released on March 30, 2005.

Protocols and Communication Standards
Web Services/ SOAP

SOAP (Simple Object Access Protocol) is a standard for exchanging XML-based messages over a computer network, normally using HTTP. SOAP forms the foundation layer of the Web services stack, providing a basic messaging framework that more abstract layers can build on.

There are several types of messaging patterns in SOAP, but by far the most common is the Remote Procedure Call (RPC) pattern, where one network node (the client) sends a request message to another node (the server), and the server immediately sends a response message to the client. More information about SOAP: http://www.w3schools.com/soap/soap_intro.asp

A **Web service** is a software system designed to support interoperable machine-to-machine interaction over a network. It has an interface described in a machine-processable format (specifically WSDL). Other systems interact with the Web service in a manner prescribed by its description using SOAP messages, typically conveyed using HTTP with an XML serialization in conjunction with other Web-related standards. Software applications written in various programming languages and running on various platforms can use Web services to exchange data over computer networks like the Internet in a manner similar to inter-process communication on a single computer. This interoperability (e.g., between Java and Python, or Windows and Linux applications) is due to the use of open standards. OASIS and the W3C are the steering committees responsible for the architecture and standardization of web services. To improve interoperability between Web service implementations, the WS-I organization has been developing a series of profiles to further define the standards involved.

CORBA — Common Object Request Broker Architecture

In computing, Common Object Request Broker Architecture (CORBA) is a standard for software componentry. The CORBA standard is created and controlled by the Object Management Group (OMG). It defines APIs, communication protocol, and object/service information models to enable heterogeneous applications written in various languages running on various platforms to interoperate. CORBA therefore provides platform and location transparency for sharing well-defined objects across a distributed computing platform.

In a general sense CORBA "wraps" code written in some language into a bundle containing additional information on the capabilities of the code inside, and how to call it. The resulting wrapped objects can then be called from other programs (or CORBA objects) over the network. In this sense, CORBA can be considered as a machine-readable documentation format, similar to a header file but with considerably more information.

RMI

The Java Remote Method Invocation API, or RMI, is a Java application programming interface for performing remote procedural calls. It is a mechanism that enables an object on one Java virtual machine to invoke methods on an object in another Java virtual machine. More information about RMI: http://java.sun.com/products/jdk/rmi/

JDBC

Java Database Connectivity, or JDBC, is an API for the Java programming language that defines how a client may access a database. It provides methods for querying and updating data in a database. JDBC is oriented towards relational databases.

JSR 170

JSR-170 is a specification developed under the Java Community Process (JCP) program.

The JSR-170 API defines how an application and a content repository interact with respect to a number of content services. For example the versioning facilities of a content repository are clearly defined, so an application knows how to browse the version history, check in and check out content items, or update and merge content in a standard fashion.

10 Advanced Taxonomy (Classification System)

Some of the material used in this chapter was first published in the *Journal of Digital Asset Management* volume 1, number 4 published by Henry Stewart Publications, London in July 2005 and is republished here with permission.

Taxonomy is the science of describing an object, in this case content or assets. In addition to describing the object, a taxonomy also places it into a relationship with other content and will group the content in logical collections or nodes of a hierarchy. A link to a website that defines the term taxonomy in more detail is: http://www.mywiseowl.com/articles/Taxonomy.

Taxonomy is not a new term, and library science is more than 2,000 years old. The current renaissance is due to a growing understanding that file systems are not the right tool to manage and control access to the growing digital content repositories of companies, governments, or any organization of even medium size. Stricter rules and regulations, specifically in the U.S., require companies to organize their content much better, and taxonomy is a way to apply some very old and proven methods to a new form of managing content. While some old wisdom can help with the new challenges, there are various aspects of the new media that are not well covered in the age-old science. This chapter will address both areas.

A taxonomy for a larger system will need to describe and group content from various sources in a logical but also useful way. This structure can become a complicated hierarchy with hundreds of nodes. If a larger system is planned and there is no librarian on staff, a company should seriously consider the services of a consultant. In addition, almost every industry conference (AIIM, Henry Stewart DAM Symposium, and others) has dedicated seminar tracks for taxonomy.

This chapter follows the order used by Ann Rockley in her outstanding book, *Managing Enterprise Content*, of distinguishing metadata between the categorization and individual data. This chapter will focus on classification or categorization of content, and Chapter 11 will provide suggestions on how to build a metadata scheme for the individual assets or content. (Ann Rockley refers to this as element metadata.)

Clarification of Terms

Before moving into more detailed description, it is recommended to clarify a few terms. This is necessary because there are no generally accepted standards or even guidelines for the terms used in describing taxonomies or data structures. (Interestingly, one will find that building a larger taxonomy is a lot about clarifying terms.)

Taxonomy is a system of describing an object also through its relationship to other objects. Usually these relationships are expressed in a hierarchy. Administrative data (use, usage rights, status, and so on) is usually not considered in these definitions. However, administrative data is very important for a system to function. The term taxonomy is also used more broadly to describe any data used to describe and classify content. It has become common to refer to any system used to find and describe digital content as taxonomy.

Metadata is a wider term, which, for the purpose of this chapter and Chapter 11, shall include any data about an object both descriptive and administrative in nature (data about data). **Metadata structure** is the system of metadata templates that will be used to classify, find, and describe the objects of a system.

Collection will refer to any grouping of content that could be a folder, collection, or a job or project.

Object will be any element that can be described with its own set of metadata: individual files, collections, folders, jobs, projects, user groups, users, upload or staging folders, and more. One way to think of an object is as a row in the database, with metadata as columns.

Authoritative term is the term used to describe a node in the classification hierarchy. An authoritative term can have many synonyms or related terms but it is chosen to represent all these concepts as the most identifiable term in the classification.

CONTINUED ▶

CONTINUED ▶

Parent/child relationship expresses the hierarchical relationship in a classification. For example, mammal is the parent of human and race is the child of human.

Ontology is a related term to taxonomy and usually explains any object from its place in the hierarchy of other objects. This chapter will avoid highly academic terms and instead use more descriptive language whenever possible.

Building the Taxonomy or Hierarchical Structure

Before starting, keep in mind that common sense is a very important element in this exercise. The end result should be a structure that is easy to use by end users, content contributors, and administrators alike. A classification system for all content of a large organization is the best-case scenario, but it just might not be practical to maintain as it requires ongoing maintenance from staff with specialized skill sets. If a key concern is a useful classification or search system for the daily tasks of the average person, then energy could be better spent on refining or "harmonizing" a number of smaller and more targeted structures managed by tools that are more departmental.

Another important clarification is that the enterprise taxonomy is not necessarily tied to a software product (existing or planned). Just as earlier chapters stressed the importance of determining the needs and parameters for enterprise content management before shopping for a software solution, it makes a lot of sense to start building the taxonomy with a piece of paper.

Mapping the Enterprise Content

As one considers what constitutes content in the organization and where it is, a classification in a hierarchical structure (taxonomy) will almost naturally start building. This structure will likely resemble the structure of any content management solutions already in use and/or the existing file systems. However, in most companies, there is no agreed upon enterprise structure to the file systems or for different content management systems, digital or otherwise. Every department has different, sometimes poorly maintained, file folders.

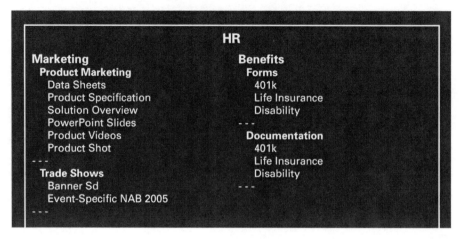

FIGURE 10.1 *A Sample Content Map*

Independent of any software solution the organization has or will employ to manage all or parts of that content, creating a map of the content in the organization, like the one in Figure 10.1, is a very valuable exercise.

Different users will make different logical associations and search for the same content in

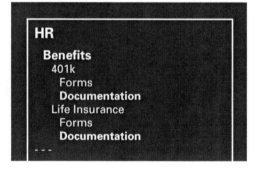

FIGURE 10.2 *An Alternative Structure*

different ways. While for the sales team "images" might include anything from photos to logos and graphics, these are very separate categories for the professional designer. In the example above it would make just as much sense to build the hierarchy based on subject matter (e.g., 401k, life insurance) than format (e.g., forms, documentation), as shown in Figure 10.2.

In the early stages of taxonomy planning, this differentiation of content versus format is not that important. The first goal is to simply identify all the content that is of value for the organization. As with any large project, it is very important to have a general understanding of the scope and context. Only after that has been established will it make sense to decide in which area more detail and organization will be of the most benefit to the organization.

As the organization thinks more about its specific situation, it will make sense to refine this general map. It is highly recommended that those doing the planning involve the people who will ultimately use this system when thinking about the following issues. This is not just general good practice but involving users is essential to capturing both the formal as well as the informal relationships and flows of content.

Short-term vs. Long-term Content

As content will be ingested or cataloged into a more organized system, it will have to follow specific rules. This can be work intensive and needs careful attention. It will most likely not be necessary to "catalog" all content. Short-lived content with minimal potential for reuse is usually not valuable enough to be cataloged. For example: Someone might carefully catalog the high resolution version of his corporate identity images. But he will probably not need to catalog every low resolution rendition, as those can easily be created on the fly by any good digital asset management system.

How deep does the system need to go?

In a library, every book gets a code that can be traced or browsed in the classification system of the library. In other words the last level of the hierarchy tree is a book as shown in Figure 10.3.

```
Technology
  Software
    Enterprise Software
      Content Management
        Ann Rockley, Managing Enterprise Content 2003, New Riders
```

FIGURE 10.3 *Classification Tree*

The ability of technology to display search results intuitively and to refine searches with specific metadata can make it a bit easier for a digital library. To use the example from Figures 10.1 and 10.2, the structure as shown in Figure 10.4 might suffice to narrow the search to just a few items that can then be displayed as a list or any other useful representation (thumbnail for example) from which any user can easily pick the desired content or asset.

Identify Non-unique Labels and Build a Unique Code

Another step to this exercise is to identify nodes in the hierarchy that have the same title or name but that do not hold the same content. An example would be

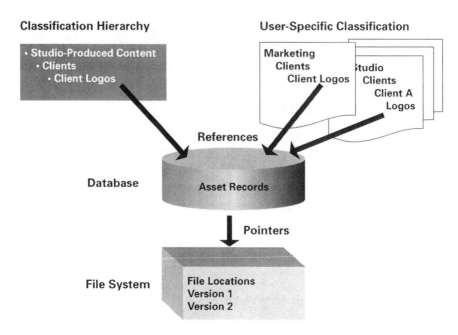

FIGURE 10.4 *Simplified Structure*

"Product Specification." A Marketing Product Spec and an Engineering Product Spec will most likely not contain the same information, but both can be found under the node Product Specification. Most software systems that will manage a hierarchy will identify the elements of that hierarchy by a unique code. As will be discussed later, this has many advantages. Therefore, it can make good sense to start thinking of a unique code scheme for the system. (MAR_PROD_SPEC and ENG_PROD_SPEC for example).

Synonyms or "Equivalence Relationships"

In addition, note all synonyms that are commonly used by target users. The best way to find out about that is to involve the users. Unfortunately, many systems fail because they are designed to fit the classification and are not built for and with the users.

In most cases, try to define the following set of data, as shown in Table 10.1:

- Unique Code

- Authoritative Term

- Synonyms, abbreviations, and maybe even common misspellings

CODE	AUTHORITATIVE TERM	SYNONYMS
MAR_PROD_SPEC	Marketing Product Specification	Product Spec, Product Specification, Data Sheet, Specs, Spec Sheet, . . .

TABLE 10.1 *Node Description*

Parallel Structures or "Polyhierarchical Taxonomies"

Typically a classification hierarchy is represented in a hierarchical, folder-like structure. However, it is important to note that different from the traditional library identification system and also from the classic computer file system, the taxonomy is not a representation of the physical location of a file or asset. The node of the hierarchy and the asset that is classified as part of that node build a relationship. Think of this system more in terms of relational databases than bookshelves.

That difference provides possibilities that the analog library cannot provide. For example, a file or asset can belong to more than one node in a hierarchy. The same book can be on different shelves simultaneously. As mentioned above, the way users will classify an object will vary on their specific perspective and need. Look at the example of an advertising agency shown in Figure 10.5:

The issue with these duplications is the maintenance of the hierarchy. If, in the example, a new version of a logo is created, it can automatically populate to all locations as long as both hierarchies are managed by the same content management tool. But if the studio creates a brand new logo for a client, it now needs to be

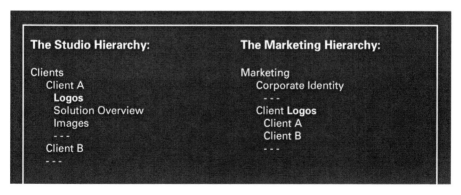

FIGURE 10.5 *Polyhierarchical Taxonomy*

updated also to the marketing "Client Logos" collection. While this can be defined as a process, it adds complexity. Therefore one must weigh the advantage of cross-reference, like the one above, against the additional administrative overhead.

Project-Based Classification

It is generally accepted that the administrator or librarian of the system can carefully maintain one authoritative classification structure. In addition to that structure, users might create specific sub-hierarchies that serve various purposes. As long as new content is also cataloged into the authoritative classification hierarchy, anybody can find it.

This system of sub-hierarchies, or project folders, also makes sense for project- or job-based collections of assets. These project folders serve a different purpose than the overall classification hierarchy. They are often short lived or created ad hoc. But they are very useful for that user or a small group of users to quickly find content in a specific context. Think of projects like "Spring Catalog" or private folders for individual users that can help them group assets or content arbitrarily for their own needs (shopping cart, light boxes, and such).

This does not duplicate files or assets. It simply references the asset in different organizational structures customized for specific purposes or users. Figure 10.6 simplifies the logical flow of that relationship between a file, the database record, and the representation through organizational hierarchies or folders.

Managing Multiple Systems with Crosswalks

In some cases one will not only duplicate the classification but will also have separate tools to manage the content. An agency's studio might use a simple image library like Canto Cumulus or Extensis Portfolio for internal organization. The agency might now try to use more sophisticated DAM tools like ClearStory's ActiveMedia or Northplain's Telescope for client-specific projects and services.

Location	Motive	Time of Year	Light	Atmosphere
Urban	Human	Spring	Sun	Fun
Outdoors	Animal	Summer	Shade	Romantic
Wild Nature	Mammal	Autumn	Half Shade	Love
- - -	- - -	Winter	- - -	- - -
		- - -		

FIGURE 10.6 *Simplified Logical Flow*

DESCRIPTION	IMAGE LIBRARY	DAM SOLUTION	MARKETING PORTAL
Name	File Name (Following original naming convention)	File Name (Following customer naming convention)	File Name (Following original naming convention)
Agency ID	N/A	File Name (Following original naming convention)	N/A
Content Descriptors	Keywords	Subjects	Keywords

TABLE 10.2 *Crosswalk Example*

Those and other more permanent duplications can be mapped with what is often called a crossover table or crosswalk.

To manage any migration from one system to another, it is necessary to map any relevant data as well. One way to do that is to create a map similar to the one in Table 10.2.

Taxonomy Management Tools

Identifying relevant and interesting content and managing that content are not necessarily tasks of the same system. After reading the prior sections, it should no surprise that there are software tools solely focused on managing taxonomies. These tools can read and feed the classification structures of various content management tools, and some even allow users to link in with other publicly available resources. The communication is mostly accomplished via WebServices or APIs.

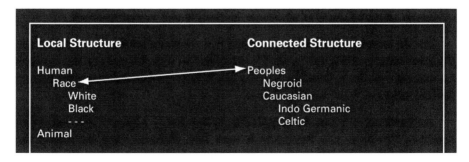

FIGURE 10.7 *Related Taxonomies*

An example would be a schoolbook publisher that is interested in the history of a specific people. The publisher's local taxonomy might have terms that are close to what he is looking for, but it might not be a good fit for people's history. A domain connected to the local domain might be more on target.

If an organization plans on this most sophisticated way to manage polyhierarchical taxonomies, it should check out companies like:

Synaptica http://www.synaptica.com/

Google (Enterprise Search Engines) http://www.google.com/enterprise/gsa/index.html

Verity http://www.verity.com/

Seth Eraley's article, "Managing Multiple Facets and Polyhierarchical Taxonomies," found at www.earley.com/Earley_Report/ER_Managing_Multiple_Taxos.htm, is great reading for the advanced user.

Using and Representing the Structure

The success of a digital content management system is measured by how much it will help users, contributors, and administrators to manage content. This will depend very much on how much the users were involved in the planning of the system (see Chapters 1 and 2 for more on this) and the quality of the user interface design and usability of the tools and systems. Taxonomy plays a great part in the usability.

There are many software tools available today that will manage classification hierarchies (taxonomies). Any document management (DM), larger Web content management (CM), or larger digital asset management (DAM) system will allow anyone to set up hierarchical structures to classify and manage content.

As just mentioned, there are also tools that are solely used to manage the classification scheme. They can be used in combination with the systems that manages the content repository. In either case the key is how the administrator can manage the hierarchy and how users can use it.

A classification hierarchy is typically represented in a hierarchical, folder-like structure. However, it is important to note that, different from the classic file system, this display is not a representation of the physical location of a file or asset.

In sophisticated systems, every node of the structure will become an object, something that can have metadata and that therefore can be searched for. Users will be able to not only browse the hierarchy, but they can also search it.

A good taxonomy tool will allow for searches such as "Spec Sheet," and the results returned depends a great deal on the work put into building the taxonomy. Unique codes and thorough synonyms allow for less specificity in the search terms that still deliver the desired search results. Following the example from earlier in the chapter, searching for "Spec Sheet" will find two codes, MAR_PROD_SPEC and ENG_PROD_SPEC, because both have "spec sheet" as a synonym of the main or authoritative term "Product Specification."

Below is a look at this search from the database perspective. The objects that the search for "Spec Sheet" would find can be expressed in simplified database rows:

UNIQUE ID	CODE	ENG_AUTH_TE RM	ENG_SYN	PARENT ID
Jh878371	MAR_PROD_S PEC	Product Specification	Product Spec, Marketing Spec, Data Sheet, Specs, Spec Sheet ...	Jh673922 (Which is the ID of Product Marketing)
Jb958403	ENG_PROD_SP EC	Product Specification	Product Spec, Product Specification , Specs, Spec Sheet, Matrix ...	AK948322 (Which is the ID of Product Documents

TABLE 10.3 *Database View of a Classification Node*

Depending on the ability and flexibility of the tool, this can result in any number of search result representation to users. One common way is this to present the root and the immediate parent of the term, as shown in Figure 10.8

In the example of a parallel structure, the search for "Logo" will provide the result as shown in Figure 10.9.

In this case the user could find the same logos in different ways, but that redundancy is not an issue as long as it is not confusing.

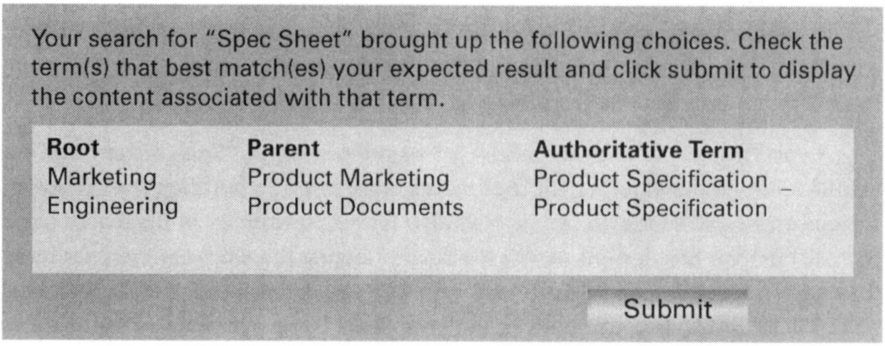

Your search for "Spec Sheet" brought up the following choices. Check the term(s) that best match(es) your expected result and click submit to display the content associated with that term.

Root	Parent	Authoritative Term
Marketing	Product Marketing	Product Specification _
Engineering	Product Documents	Product Specification

Submit

FIGURE 10.8 *Root–Parent Display*

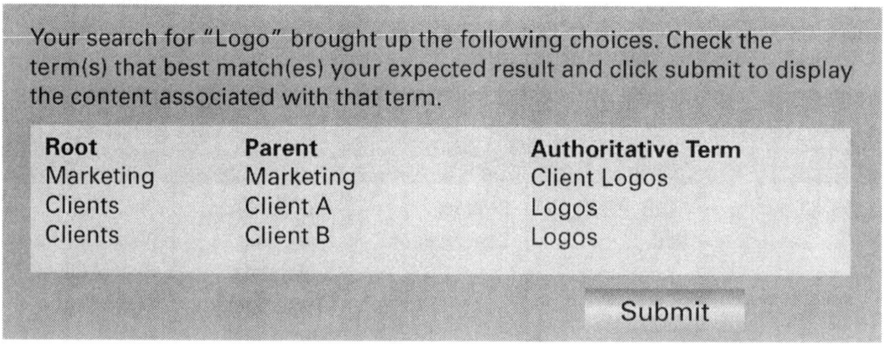

Your search for "Logo" brought up the following choices. Check the term(s) that best match(es) your expected result and click submit to display the content associated with that term.

Root	Parent	Authoritative Term
Marketing	Marketing	Client Logos
Clients	Client A	Logos
Clients	Client B	Logos

Submit

FIGURE 10.9 *Parallel Root–Parent Display*

Multi Language

The concept of hierarchy objects that are identified by unique codes is also the key to Multilanguage display. A database might represent an object like shown in table 10.4.

UNIQUE ID	CODE	ENG_AUTH_TERM	ENG_SYN	GER_AUTH_TERM	GER_SYN
Jh878371	MAR_PROD_SPEC	Product Specification	Spec Sheet	Technische Produkt Broschüre	Technische Daten Beschreibung

TABLE 10.4 *Database View of Classification Node*

This would allow a user to search for the term "Spec Sheet" in German: "Technische Daten Beschreibung" and find the same content because that content has a relationship to the classification term identified by the language neutral Unique ID "Jh878371."

Subject Domains and Synonyms

Similar to the display elements above, a good interface of an advanced taxonomy management tools should provide options to explore a term in a hierarchy. In addition to parent and children, this interface should display synonyms, links to related terms of connected domains, and possibly translations into forging languages.

Summary

For a larger system, just defining the basic taxonomy can take weeks. There is no reason to wait until a decision for a product or vendor has been made. This classification will be a very useful tool for any vendor or consultant who will work on the system.

Above all else, use common sense when building the taxonomy. While many companies are realizing that content management on the enterprise level is a key strategy for long term success, a simple inventory with a well thought through structure is a good first step. However, classification is only one step of the process. In most cases users will not traverse long, potentially complex hierarchies to look for content. They will want to search by typing same basic values in a search page. This kind of search will require metadata, covered in Chapter 11.

11 Metadata

Some of the material used in this chapter was first published in the *Journal of Digital Asset Management* volume 1, number 4 published by Henry Stewart Publications, London in July 2005 and is republished here with permission.

This chapter will provide suggestions for building a metadata structure and for the processes of assigning metadata to content. The concepts and issues discussed in this chapter are closely related to those discussed in Chapter 10. If the reader is new to the topic of metadata then the section on Clarification of Terms in Chapter 10 should be consulted prior to reading this chapter.

The later part of this chapter describes considerations in regard to data structures not commonly included in the taxonomy discussions. These data structures include user groups and roles, security, ingestion and download, folder structures, as well as other searchable indexes.

Simplified, metadata is data which that will be used to describe and most importantly to find the file. There are different schools of thought about how to group that data. Metadata can be:

- Information about the file (objective): File size, type, color space, bit rate, and so on

- Information about the content (subjective or user-defined): Author, location, target audience, topic, and so on

- Administrative information: Approval status, storage path, lifecycle status, use, and so on

- Information about the file's relationships: Collections, parent documents, projects, jobs, inclusions, and so on

Building Metadata Templates

Anyone working on building metadata templates will find that different objects will need different data to be described and classified. A video's encoding type and compression are important, while MS Word documents will not need that information, but a value like "number of pages" might be helpful.

A list of common data types and explanations is provided in this chapter's section, "Common Data Types." If the system grows larger, a hierarchical composition of metadata templates for different categories of content may make sense. The Figure 11.1 shows an example.

In this example, an MS Word document would have the following data: Classification ID, Notes, Keywords, File Type, Author, Topic, Page Count, Last Printed.

As with all other aspects of introducing a new or expanded digital content management system, planning is a very important first step. The metadata structure should stem from the taxonomy set forth for the system. See Chapter 10 for more details on taxonomies. Following are a number of questions that can help when building the metadata structure.

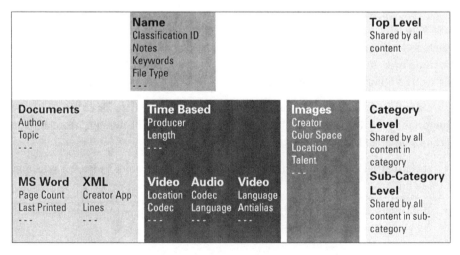

FIGURE 11.1 *Hierarchical Composition of Metadata Templates*

What Metadata to Assign?

The key question is what data is needed to assign to the different kinds of content or assets. There are three considerations when developing

- **What data is needed for users and administrators to find an object?**
  Users are not only internal staff, but can be channel partners, consumers, investors, and the press. It will often make sense to clarify which user group will use which data to find assets.

- **What data is needed to provide information about the object that users need but that is not used for searches?**
  This could be the file size or general notes.

- **What data might be needed in the future to find content or objects in an archive or in the later stages of its life cycle versus the earlier stages?**
  It might make sense to assign just a small set of data to an asset initially, because time is of the essence. A fast turnaround of assets from a live event is one example. Some of these assets might later become part of more permanent libraries and need additional metadata, such as key words or usage descriptions.

How Much Data Can One Handle?

There is a big difference between the data that can be assigned versus the data that is really needed by the users. There is a limit on how much data the average user and also the administrators can work with. It is just as critical to see that metadata is not "overassigned," wasting administrative time and possibly confusing or distracting users, as it is to ensure that the right data is assigned.

How Much Data Can the Users Handle?

Many systems fail because the search pages are designed with dozens of options and qualifiers. Most often less is more. Only few people have ever used the advanced search features of Google. Most users have limited time and even shorter patience. In order to become a useful tool, any system needs to be easy to use. Some complexity can be overcome by good search UI design (discussed later in this chapter), but there is a limit to how much data a user can be expected to provide to find the content they look for. This also depends on the level of sophistication and training.

How Much Data Can the Administrators Handle?

There are options to support the administrator or librarian in keeping order with metadata, classification, and cross-references. These options are described in the next section. In many cases, manual controls are necessary to keep the data "clean" and to ensure searches reliably return all applicable objects. Therefore, the administrator or librarian has an important job, which the section about data integrity will describe below. As the system is designed, one must ensure that the administrative tasks are not becoming overwhelming or a bottleneck of the system's efficiency. Of course, it is not solely the librarian who applies metadata. The processes of who assigns what data should be well-defined and include the staff with the best context and motivation.

How Is the Data Assigned or Applied?

As defined above there are different kinds of metadata. Below are the four categories and definitions of who and how the data is applied. The task of assigning the correct data is often a collaborative effort.

Information about the file (objective): File size, type, color space, bit rate, and so on

This data can often be extracted automatically. That is good, but unfortunately this data is the least useful in identifying a specific file or asset. This data would be an "advanced" search option or is simply information provided to users after they have found the content.

Information about the content (subjective or user-defined): Author, location, target audience, topic

Arguably this data is the most valuable for finding an asset by search terms. In most cases, some of the subjective data is best provided by the content creator or someone very familiar with the content's context. Caption text of a photo or keywords describing the content, for example, are best defined by people closer to the context than the system administrator or general librarian. It could be the job of the latter to ensure data has been assigned in the right format, but it is often hard for those not familiar with the content to ensure the descriptive data is correct. Data about the content that has to do with business rules, such as owner or usage rights, can then often be defined by more administrative roles. Administrative information can be used to manage that workflow.

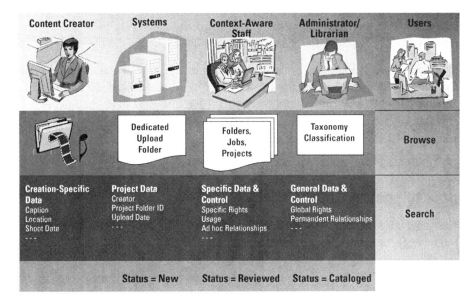

Content Creator | Systems | Context-Aware Staff | Administrator/ Librarian | Users

| | Dedicated Upload Folder | Folders, Jobs, Projects | Taxonomy Classification | Browse |

Creation-Specific Data	Project Data	Specific Data & Control	General Data & Control	
Caption	Creator	Specific Rights	Global Rights	
Location	Project Folder ID	Usage	Permanent Relationships	Search
Shoot Date	Upload Date	Ad hoc Relationships	...	
...	...	...		

Status = New   Status = Reviewed   Status = Cataloged

FIGURE 11.2 *Sample Classification and Metadata Assignment Steps*

Administrative information: Aapproval status, storage path, life cycle status, use and so on

This data is either controlled by the system or by more administrative roles. A typical set up would be to automatically tag any newly ingested file with a certain status, for example "New." This will then allow a dedicated librarian, information architect, or other dedicated role to search for data with a "New" status, perform the necessary tasks, and set the applicable status for the next step, for example "Reviewed." Figure 11.2 is an illustration of a sample content flow through the different classification and metadata assignment steps.

If the organization is large and has a well-defined content management strategy with a defined enterprise taxonomy, a dedicated role to control or manage that aspect may already be in place.

Information about the file's relationships: Collections, parent documents, projects, jobs, inclusions, and so on

As shown in the illustration above, this data can be assigned by the system automatically, for example, by using a dedicated upload folder that will assign predefined relationships to a project folder. Other examples include the upload of compound documents like QuarkXPress or InDesign. Those documents consist of many files that any good DAM system will link automatically in a parent/child relationship.

Throughout the content life cycle, an asset or file might be assigned to other collections, folders, jobs, and the like by users or administrators, as discussed in "Project-Based Classification" in Chapter 10. This will most likely happen manually. One key issue is how to ensure all this data and the relationships will be useful and not confusing due to errors, omissions, or misclassifications. Data integrity is an important issue.

How to Ensure Data Integrity?

The prior section discussed options to automate the assignment of metadata. However, there is always a degree of human intervention necessary to fully classify and describe specifically visually rich content. Content management requires dedication and skill. Therefore, the processes defined for the assignment of data are very important. A basic rule is that there should be an incentive for the person assigning the data to do so with careful attention. Another aspect of data integrity is control.

No library would expect the average user to file books back onto the shelf. The margin of error would be too high. To follow the example from Figure 11.2, the average creative worker can be expected to provide data vital for his/her work and to drop the file into a dedicated hot folder, but one should not expect anything more.

Managing content should be defined and articulated as part of the job description of the staff, such as information architects (IA) and librarians (sometimes also called cybrarians), that is responsible for setting up hot folders and assigning key data. These jobs require dedication and skill. One common reason why systems do not archive to the expected effectiveness is because companies underestimate this aspect and leave the crucial management of metadata and relationships to unqualified and poorly trained staff. The level of data integrity — and therefore the effectiveness of the system — is equivalent to the dedication and skill of the staff in charge of managing it. Technology has only a limited role in this aspect. The catchphrase "Garbage in, Garbage out," has never been more applicable. If the cost of qualified staff is not part of the calculations for the projected return on investment, the calculations are flawed.

One tool that can be used to ensure data integrity by administrators is that of controlled vocabulary, defining a group of values from which users choose the appropriate data rather than just entering free text. This ensures a consistency and completeness as metadata is assigned across the enterprise. There are various ways to configure this controlled vocabulary. They can be in the form of lists, hierarchies (again), or other controls. Both the value and the format of information can be controlled to some degree. While this can help ensure data is assigned correctly, the process will need additional thought and planning on the part of the system administrators. In the list of common data types in this chapter, the controlled vocabulary options are highlighted.

There are various measures that an administrator or librarian can take to ensure that metadata was assigned and was assigned correctly. Figure 11.2 outlines two control steps in the process. If the control is not part of the metadata assignment tasks at time of cataloging, an administrator can simply search for an Ingestion or Catalog Date Range and inspect submitted material randomly or systematically (every tenth cataloged file, for example).

Most systems will also allow searching for omissions. For example, a librarian could search for all content that does not have a classification ID. This is as important as reviewing the data that is assigned.

Control is also a task that can be distributed to the areas of the organization that have a stake in certain aspects of the system. For example, the marketing department could and should have a dedicated person who will check for new logos created by the studio and add them to the Marketing Client Logos folder, for example.

While control and data integrity are very important for the usefulness and the adoption of the new tools and processes, an even more important element is the presentation of both search options and the resulting information and content.

How Is the Data Represented?

This is a very important question — the UI is the ultimate milestone by which the usefulness of the system will be measured. The Resource section includes sources for more in-depth information.

To address user needs sufficiently, a system will need a way to build UIs (even a medium-size system will have probably more than one) that are flexible and adaptable. It also needs to accommodate some freedom of creativity on the side of the designers. Most out-of-the-box designs are targeted at one specific use case. If a tool does not provide some level of freedom in creating "customized" UIs, it is not a good tool for an enterprise application of any kind.

The graphics used to depict hierarchies in this chapter, for example, are all very dry and boring. There is no need to represent a hierarchy in that way. Images or any more visual elements can become an intuitive and "fun" way to navigate. Fun is not necessarily a standard design guideline but should certainly be considered. Flash and many other technologies allow users to move and adjust components on a Web site, thus creating a personalized experience that can actually be fun. This is a very important element of engaging the user and is an invaluable contribution to the user acceptance, which in turn, contributes to the success of the entire project.

In general there are three kinds of interfaces to think about:

- Search Interfaces

- Information Display Interfaces (search results)

- Administrative or Editing Interfaces

Search Interfaces

A search actually starts before a user arrives at a search interface. It starts the moment a user clicks on a bookmark, enters a URL, or chooses a specific application to look for something. Therefore, it is important to include these choices when analyzing the best interface approach for any system.

When a user needs to pick a geographical location, for example, this can be displayed in a long list or as an interactive map or animated globe that the user can click. The globe is sure to engage users much more intuitively. They might not even consider this "searching." After the user has arrived in California, the search option could include entering a search term in a Google-like style or add some "advanced" data values (dates, file type, or such).

Saved searches are also a great tool to make it easier for users to find specific assets. A saved search can define even a very complex query and present it as a simple link on an intranet site, for example. Think of an example link on a marketing page: "New logos and graphics for use in Power Point presentations." A link like this can hide the complexity of a specific query for example: <Collection= Marketing_Client_LogosORMarketing_New_Product_ Graphics&Resolution=low_ res&Status=Approved>

Information Display

How information is displayed is another important aspect of a good system. As with general interface design, the more targeted the information is for a specific

User Role Title:
Marketing

Images
Presentation: Low-res thumbnail and at least one enlargement
(No need to zoom or pan)
Information: Color space, file size, file type, resolution, marketing

FIGURE 11.3 *UI Specific User Group Definition*

user or use case, the better. When building display interfaces for users, it is essential to know what the users need to know, including understanding both the kind of data that is required as well as the best format for that data. The various metadata types and formats that are commonly used will be examined later. The content itself can also have various renditions or proxies.

The most successful systems are those where planners and administrators have created a matrix of each user group and their requirements, such as the one in Figure 11.3.

Administrative

Administrators or librarians often have very different needs from the average user. At the same time, they should also spend more time in training and therefore should have a much better understanding of what the system can do. In some cases, an administrative interface is not a Web browser but a thick client, where the application is installed on a local computer. This allows more sophisticated actions, such as batch uploads and batch assignment of data or also editing of end-user interfaces.

A good system should allow administrators to build search pages on the fly by selecting from dozens of possible search values. These searches can hopefully be saved for reuse or even published as links to the end user.

User and application security is another aspect of the administrator interface. Integration with exiting user administration tools such as iPlanet, Microsoft Active Directory, or other LPAD-based products is not the final answer to this issue. Many application-specific user administration tasks will have to be performed in any larger content management system. Access control and security will also impact the taxonomy planning.

Common Data Types

Descriptive

- Pick one or pick many lists
These lists allow for controlled vocabulary. The biggest advantage of this data form is that it ensures the correct entry and spelling as well as consistency. It can be limiting if the list is not well defined. Systems can be configured to allow users to add to a list.
- Numeric (numbers, dates, currency)
- Alphanumeric (codes and unique IDs)
- Yes/No (or Boolean)
- In this case it is important to verify that a system can also handle omissions. Administrators might need to search for assets where no value was assigned.
- Free text field
This presents the most risk for user error and misspelling but is common for notes, keywords, and caption.
- Controlled text fields
Users can control the length or format of entered text. For example users can check for the name@domainname.xxx e-mail address format or (XXX) XXX-XXXX for a phone number with area code. Predefining these controlled text fields ensures consistency in the data format as many users add data to the system.
- Hierarchical (with or without inheritance)
Data types that are best expressed in a hierarchical manner are often overlapping into the classification area. However, it can make sense to allow users to pick one or multiple values from a hierarchical structure other than the main taxonomy. Inheritance means that a lower level value will automatically inherit the values of the nodes above. A human is always also a mammal. That inheritance flows down the tree, but inheritance can flow the other way around. Non-inheriting structures are more like computer file systems. Users only get the value they pick.
A good example for hierarchical inheriting metadata is keywords for image libraries. When looking for an image, hierarchies like these can be a great tool like shown in Figure 11.4.

CONTINUED ▶

CONTINUED ▶

Location	Motive	Time of Year	Light	Atmosphere
Urban	Human	Spring	Sun	Fun
Outdoors	Animal	Summer	Shade	Romantic
Wild Nature	Mammal	Autumn	Half Shade	Love
- - -	- - -	Winter	- - -	- - -
		- - -		

Figure 11.4 *Metadata Hierarchies*

Relationships

In addition to descriptive and administrative metadata, there are various relationships that can be important:

- Containers
  - Collections
  - Folders
  - Jobs
  - Projects

  These containers for content or assets are objects that can be searched and organized just as individual assets can.
- Parent/Child

  An HTML page, a QuarkXPress, or Adobe InDesign document consists usually of a master template and various linked files.
- Lineage

  This relationship usually tracks reuse as in a composite image (a new image created out of multiple photos) or between renditions that became individual assets. It is a mix of parent/child and peer-to-peer.
- Versioning

  This is mostly a sequential linear relationship but can become a complex relationship between different versions of a file and versions of the metadata. Versions can become hierarchical tree structures if different versions continue to evolve in parallel.
- Peer-to-peer

  This relationship links assets without creating a new object like a folder or collection. An example is the domain relationship discussed earlier in this chapter: Race is related to People.

What Needs Metadata?

As a final area of planning, it will be necessary to think about the different elements that need metadata. Those elements are defined as objects. Most of this chapter focused on the classification and description of content. But there are other objects that will need to be classified and grouped, and often they need metadata for searching and administrative tasks.

Here is a list of the most common elements that will most likely have to be included in the planning process:

- Files/Content/ Assets
  - Versions

- Containers
  - Collections
  - Folders
  - Jobs
  - Projects

- Users

- User Groups

- Roles

- Upload or Staging Folders

- Nodes of the taxonomy tree (sometimes called subjects)
  As mentioned earlier, a node of taxonomy can become an object which can be searched and which can have metadata such as synonyms and translations.

Testing

In the planning for a larger system, one should consider testing the system on a smaller scale. This is not always easy because with limited content, the users will often not find anything when searching for specific items. This defeats the purpose of providing a realistic testing environment. Therefore, effective pilot projects are quite difficult to realize. A phased implementation approach is often the best alternative. Start with building an image library, for example, or enable access for just one client through the services portal. The best first phases are those which are complete implementations with limited but well-defined scope. They can provide valuable feedback and with that build the competency of everyone involved over time.

Access Control and Application Security

One area that deserves mention is not usually considered as part of the taxonomy or metadata structure: access control and application security.

Even in a mid-size system of a few thousand assets, a user can be overwhelmed with the search options and the information that is available. Access control is not only a way to ensure that assets are not accessed by unauthorized users, but it is also a way to hide some complexity from the users. They will only see what makes sense to them. For example a sales person will want the PDF of the marketing brochure. They do not need the native QuarkXPress file of the same name, and they surely don't need to see all the linked files that make up the end result. By assigning access right according to roles, the information can be filtered to the most applicable set of content.

Summary

The implementation of content management systems is best accomplished in phasesand it is no different for complex taxonomy and metadata structures. As mentioned in Chapter 10, the future data structure can begin to take shape in the form of a spreadsheet or table. The implementation and refinement of the details can be accomplished in phases. These phases should not be isolated projects. They should follow a larger strategy or vision, but with each phase this data model can and most likely will be adjusted to reflect "lessons learned."

Appendix

LABOR TASKS (MINUTES)	MANUAL	AUTO-MATED	NOTES
Find and retrieve 35 ads and collateral pieces for each product group	480	35	Find ads on network and workstations — engage colleagues for assistance *DAM search by product & campaign allows rapid access*
Find and retrieve marketing plan, creative briefs, communication plan, and performance reports	240	30	May entail extensive data analyses, requests made to staff and agencies, and updates & addenda *DAM search by product, campaign, and team allows rapid access*
Collect, organize, and package materials	210	10	Aggregate files, draft index and instructions, burn CD or post to FTP site *DAM system assigns asset to a unique collection — accessible globally*
Distribute package to review team	120	5	Correspond with team members, label and ship CDs or email FTP instructions *DAM system messages team members with link to established collection*

LABOR TASKS (MINUTES)	MANUAL	AUTO-MATED	NOTES
Conduct team review, markup, and editing	360	60	Hold in person meetings, phone conferences, extended email threads *DAM system manages participant markup and non-linear change tracking*
Acquire final approval, lock package	60	15	Review and discuss via email, phone with approver *DAM system tags final collection as "approved"*
Reworks due to errors	120	0	Inappropriate source materials, poor versioning
Subtotal (minutes)	**1590**	**155**	Time required to complete and distribute ONE collection
CYCLE TIME			
Calendar days required to complete	12	2	Per distribution of ONE collection

LABOR COSTS ($)	MANUAL	AUTO-MATED	DIFFERENCE BASED ON PORTION OF WORK COMPLETED BY EACH ACTOR
Chief marketing officer (CMO)	$ 100.00	$ 50.00	$1,000 per hour fully-burdened rate
Marketing manager	$ 11.25	$ 22.50	$75 per hour fully-burdened rate
Project specialist, contractor	$ 7.50	22.50	$75 per hour fully-burdened rate
Agency creative director	$ 37.50	$ 25.00	$250 per hour billing rate
Agency account supervisor	$ 33.00	$ 8.25	$165 per hour billing rate
Agency traffic manager	$ 22.00	$ 11.00	$110 per hour billing rate

LABOR COSTS ($)	MANUAL	AUTO-MATED	DIFFERENCE BASED ON PORTION OF WORK COMPLETED BY EACH ACTOR
Agency production assistant	$ 10.00	$ 10.00	$100 per hour billing rate
Blended labor rate	$ 221.25	$ 149.25	Represents proportional hourly rate of team involved
Labor Costs Subtotal	$ 5,863	$ 386	Per review and distribution of ONE collection

MATERIAL COSTS ($)	MANUAL	AUTO-MATED	NOTES
Physical media (CD/DVD)	$ 3.00	$ -	CDs burned by marketing manager $0.60 per CD
Freight, courier, express mail	$ 34.00	$ -	4 mailings at $8.50 average corporate rate
Agency billing (ship, process)	$ 75.00	$ -	3 mailings by agency at $25 service fee each
Material Costs Subtotal	$ 112.00	$ -	Per distribution of ONE collection

ANNUAL COSTS ($) MANUAL	MANUAL	AUTO-MATED	NOTES
Reviews per year	6	6	
Annual labor costs	$ 35,179	$ 2,313	
Annual material costs	$ 672	$ -	
Incremental DAM utility cost	$ -	$ 3,024	Given 125 users, 5-year cost recovery model, and $270K system cost
Total Annual Costs	$ 35,851	$ 5,337	

ECONOMIC GAINS ($)	SAVINGS	PERCENT	
Total labor savings	$ 32,865	93.42%	Percent reduction in costs, auto-mated vs. manual
Total material cost savings	$ 672	100.00%	Percent reduction in costs, auto-mated vs. manual
Total Economic Gain	**$ 35,851**		

INTANGIBLE GAINS	VALUE	EFFECT	
Cycle time	60	Days gained in time to market for this content per year	
Stakeholder service	30%	More stakeholders served with this content per year	
Brand touch-points	50%	More brand touch points fulfilled by this content per year	
Brand consistency infractions	85%	Fewer off-brand messages with this content per year	
Legal compliance infractions	95%	Fewer compliance infractions related to this content per year	

TABLE A.1 *A Bottom Up ROI Calculation*

TOP DOWN RETURN ON INVESTMENT MODEL FOR A DIGITAL CONTENT MANAGEMENT SOLUTION IN A GLOBAL MARKETING DEPARTMENT

Assumptions:
$100M total global marketing expenditures
Fast to moderate revenue cycle-time firm — consumer products

Item	Value	Notes
Marketing expenditures	$50,000,000	50% of global spend
Breakdown of expenditure by functional area		

	Total Portion	Internal Portion	Internal Costs	External Spend	External Spend	Total Costs
Strategy/Planning	8%	70%	$ 2,800,000	30%	$ 1,200,000	$ 4,000,000
Localization Work	20%	10%	$ 1,000,000	90%	$ 9,000,000	$10,000,000
Creative Work	18%	5%	$ 450,000	95%	$ 8,550,000	$ 9,000,000
Account Services & Vendor Management	7%	89%	$ 3,115,000	11%	$ 385,000	$ 3,500,000
Digital Production — Web, Multimedia & Interactive	25%	25%	$ 3,125,000	75%	$ 9,375,000	$12,500,000
Production — Print	35%	1%	$ 175,000	99%	$17,325,000	$17,500,000
Totals	**113%**		**$10,665,000**		**$45,835,000**	**$56,500,000**

CONTINUED ►

TOP DOWN RETURN ON INVESTMENT MODEL FOR A DIGITAL CONTENT MANAGEMENT SOLUTION IN A GLOBAL MARKETING DEPARTMENT

Percentage of overall cost related to staff working with assets

	Concept	Create	Manage	Distribute	Localize	Consume	Analyze & Archive	Sum	Percent of Total
Strategy/Planning	15%	4%	5%	3%	2%	3%	2%	34%	7%
Localization Work	2%	8%	7%	4%	55%	5%	2%	83%	18%
Creative Work	9%	25%	8%	12%	15%	1%	5%	75%	16%
Account Services & Vendor Management	5%	8%	20%	6%	30%	1%	10%	80%	18%
Digital Production — Web, Multimedia & Interactive	2%	30%	12%	12%	22%	20%	2%	100%	22%
Production - Print	1%	32%	15%	6%	26%	1%	5%	86%	19%

CONTINUED ▶

TOP DOWN RETURN ON INVESTMENT MODEL FOR A DIGITAL CONTENT MANAGEMENT SOLUTION IN A GLOBAL MARKETING DEPARTMENT

Dollar Amount of overall cost related to staff working with assets

	Concept	Create	Manage	Distribute	Localize	Consume	Analyze & Archive	Lifecycle Related Expenditures	Expenditures Not Marcom Lifecycle Related
Strategy/Planning	$ 600,000	$ 160,000	$ 200,000	$ 120,000	$ 80,000	$ 120,000	$ 80,000	$ 1,360,000	
Localization Services	$ 200,000	$ 800,000	$ 700,000	$ 400,000	$ 5,500,000	$ 500,000	$ 200,000	$ 8,300,000	
Creative Services	$ 810,000	$ 2,250,000	$ 720,000	$ 1,080,000	$ 1,350,000	$ 90,000	$ 450,000	$ 6,750,000	
Account Services & Vendor Management	$ 175,000	$ 280,000	$ 700,000	$ 210,000	$ 1,050,000	$ 35,000	$ 350,000	$ 2,800,000	
Digital Production - Web, Multimedia & Interactive	$ 250,000	$ 3,750,000	$ 1,500,000	$ 1,500,000	$ 2,750,000	$ 2,500,000	$ 250,000	$12,500,000	
Production - Print	$ 175,000	$ 5,600,000	$ 2,625,000	$ 1,050,000	$ 4,550,000	$ 175,000	$ 875,000	$15,050,000	
TOTAL	$ 2,210,000	$12,840,000	$ 6,445,000	$ 4,360,000	$15,280,000	$ 3,420,000	$ 2,205,000	$46,760,000	$ 3,240,000
%	5%	28%	14%	9%	33%	7%	5%	83%	6%

CONTINUED

TOP DOWN RETURN ON INVESTMENT MODEL FOR A DIGITAL CONTENT MANAGEMENT SOLUTION IN A GLOBAL MARKETING DEPARTMENT

Percentage of cost impact of the digital content management solution on staff activities

	Customization & Localization Work	Global Digital Content Store	Marketing Best Practices	Department Content Portal	Ecommerce	Access Control & Content Licensing	On-Demand Transformation Services	Total	Percent of Total
Concept	3%	5%	14%	0%	0%	14%	0%	36%	9%
Create	2%	13%	8%	9%	15%	10%	25%	82%	21%
Manage	10%	25%	0%	5%	10%	16%	3%	69%	18%
Distribute	0%	5%	0%	20%	28%	3%	14%	70%	18%
Localize	35%	4%	2%	14%	15%	7%	12%	89%	23%
Consume	0%	5%	0%	8%	16%	0%	19%	48%	12%
Analyze & Archive	1%	18%	1%	6%	12%	0%	4%	42%	

CONTINUED ►

TOP DOWN RETURN ON INVESTMENT MODEL FOR A DIGITAL CONTENT MANAGEMENT SOLUTION IN A GLOBAL MARKETING DEPARTMENT

Dollar amount of cost impact of the digital content management solution on staff activities. In a perfect world, with the perfect execution, what of these costs could be avoided?

	Customization & Localization Work	Global Digital Content Store	Marketing Best Practices	Department Content Portal	Ecommerce	Access Control & Content Licensing	On-Demand Transformation Services	Potential Affected Expenditures	Expenditures Not Related to Content Mgmt
Concept	$ 66,300	$ 110,500	$ 309,400	$ 0	$ 0	$ 309,400	$ 0	$ 795,600	
Create	256,800	1,669,200	1,027,200	1,155,600	1,926,000	1,284,000	3,210,000	10,528,800	
Manage	644,500	1,611,250	0	322,250	644,500	1,031,200	193,350	4,447,050	
Distribute	0	218,000	0	872,000	1,220,800	130,800	610,400	3,052,000	
Localize	5,348,000	611,200	305,600	2,139,200	2,292,000	1,069,600	1,833,600	13,599,200	
Consume	0	171,000	0	273,600	547,200	0	649,800	1,641,600	
Analyze & Archive	22,050	396,900	22,050	132,300	264,600	0	88,200	926,100	
TOTAL	$ 6,337,650	$ 4,788,050	$ 1,664,250	$ 4,894,950	$ 6,895,100	$ 3,825,000	$ 6,585,350	$ 34,990,350	$ 11,769,650
%	18%	14%	5%	14%	20%	11%	19%	75%	25%

TABLE A.2 *A Bottom Down ROI Calculation*

Index

A

ActiveMedia 114
Adobe Creative Suite xv, 92, 95, 99
Adobe Graphic Server (AGS) xv, 27
application program interfaces (API) 86–87,
        100, 102–103
  capabilities 88
  Java remote method invocation (RMI)
      100
  limitations 88
  simple object access protocol (SOAP)
      100
application design 40
architecture, general 85
  n-tier back end architecture 85
  services oriented architecture (SOA) 85
architectural concepts and terms 102
  application program interface (API) 102
  services oriented architecture (SOA) 102
  software development kit (SDK) 102
assembly tools 26–27, 45
asset management engine 22
authentication 43, 47, 51, 55, 90, 99
authoring tools 33
authoritative term 108, 112–113, 117–118
  definition 108

B

brand resource management (BRM) 21
business intelligence 22
business logic 83–84, 92–93
business process automation 34, 44, 83
business transaction engine 23

C

Canto Cumulus 114
CanWest MediaWorks 63
  case study 63
change management 9–10, 13–14, 20, 32,
       57, 72, 79, 81
  organizational change 16
  user involvement 15
chief knowledge officer (CKO) 18
classification hierarchies (taxonomies) 116
classification node 117–118
classification system 9, 62, 100, 107, 109,
      111
  advanced 107
classification tree 111
ClearStory Systems 30, 114
collaboration engine 23
collection 17, 107–108, 122, 125, 131–132
  definition 108

compliance xi, 7, 47, 51, 54–56, 59, 67, 80, 101
  access security 53
  HIPPA 51
  requirement to produce a record 51
  requirement to prove who accessed a record and when 53
  requirement to provide a certain version and metadata of a record 52
  Sarbanes-Oxley 51–52, 59
  usage tracking 53
  write once read many (WORM) storage technology 52
content flow 33, 39, 62, 125
  sample content flow chart 39
content life cycle 6, 126
content management (CM) 18, 27, 116
  defined 27
  hierarchical structures 116
  logical flow 28
  tools and processes 27
content management engine 22
content management system (CMS) 19, 52
  business logic 83
    definition 83
  business process automation 44, 83–84
  version tracking 52
  web-based 77
Content Manager 30
copyright 47–48, 50, 53–55, 80
Corbis xv, 54–55
  case study 54
  digital watermarking 55
core application 43, 84, 86, 88, 92, 94
  vendor 89
  open source 91
  performance 90
  pricing 89
creator applications 33, 99
crossover table 114–115
crosswalk 114–115
  example 115
customer relationship management (CRM) 22

D
data structure 5–6, 108, 121, 133
database 22–23, 43, 73, 84, 86, 92–93, 99, 106, 108, 112–114, 117–118
design considerations 85
Digimarc ImageBridge™ 55
Digimarc MarcSpider™ 55

digital asset management (DAM) xiii, 1, 16–17, 21, 25, 37, 116
  brand resource management (BRM) 21
  director 17
  hierarchical structures 116
  logical flow 26
  manager 17
  marketing content management (MCM) 21
  media asset management (MAM) 21
  tools and processes 25–26
digital content xi– xiii
  authentication 47
  compliance 47
  copyright 47
  digital rights management (DRM) 47
  usage rights restriction 47
digital content management (DCM) xiii– xv, 1, 7, 30, 55, 59, 80, 97
  business transaction engine 23
  change management 13–14
  collaboration engine 23
  complex 13, 20
  content or asset management engine 22
  creative and editorial tools 99–100
  evolving competencies 13, 17
  expansion 57, 62
    defining 5, 11
    design considerations 85
    direction 1
    flexibility 8
    hardware 83, 96
    horizontal expansion 7
    integration options 8
    profit 58
    reasons to expand 1, 57
    risk assessment 62
    scalability 8
    scale in size 5
    software 83, 96
    starting point 1
    strategy 58
    vertical expansion 6
    vision 58
  governance models 13, 17–18, 57, 72
  industry xiii, 18

integration 97
  business processes 101
  creative and editorial tools 99
  digital content management 97
  digital content production 97
  digital rights management 97
  financial transaction and subscription
    management 97
  licenses/agreements management
    (B2B) 97
  supply chain management 97
  use and user data aggregation (CRM)
    97
limits of technology 13
managers and administrators 10
metadata and relationship index 22
organizational change 16
search engine 23
security logic 23
system definition 33
  application design 33, 40
  assembly and manipulation tools 33,
    45
  business process integration 33, 44
  content flow 33
  file types 33
  structured versus unstructured
    content 33
  system architecture 33, 41
  system security 40
  UI (user interface) requirements 33, 40
  use cases for user groups and roles 33
  user/security administration 33
  workflow or business process
    automation 33, 44
  user involvement 15
  workflow engine 23
digital content production 97
digital media enterprise xi, xiv, 97–98
digital media platform (DMP) 30
digital rights management 22, 47, 55, 90,
    97, 99
  digital rights management technology 50
digital watermarking 55
document management (DM) 1, 21, 23, 116
  definition 23
  hierarchical structures 116
  logical flow 25
  tools and processes 24
document type definition (DTD) 38
Dreamweaver xv, 27, 92

E
e-commerce 22–23, 27–29, 78, 98–99
e-mail management 22
electronic news production system for TV
    news (ENPS) xv, 39, 99
enterprise architecture 98–100
  application services, middleware, or
    framework layer 98
  core services layer 98
  data layer 99
  presentation layer 98
enterprise content management (ECM) xiii,
    19, 21, 28
  building 29
  defined 28
  logical flow 29
enterprise media server (EMS) 30
enterprise resource management (ERM) 22
enterprise services platform 98
extended markup language (XML) 38, 100
Extensis Portfolio 114

F
Fernseh Data Base (FDB) 4
file types 36
  sample file matrix for images 37
Final Cut Pro xv, 26, 95, 99
Firefox xv, 95

G
governance models 13, 17–18, 20, 57, 72
graphical user interface (GUI) 104

H
Harcourt, Inc. 16
  case study 18
hardware 83
hierarchical storage management (HSM) 27,
    94
hierarchical structure (taxonomy) 109, 116,
    129
  authoritative term 112
  building 109
  content map 110
  identify non-unique labels 111
  manage content 116
  short-term vs. long-term 111
  synonyms 112
  unique code 111–112
HIPPA 51
HP 30

I
IBM 30
InDesign xv, 25, 38, 125, 131
intellectual property (IP) xiii, 17–18, 59
intellectual property resource (IPR) 17
iPlanet 43, 129
iterative planning 10

J
Java remote method invocation (RMI) 100
Journal of Digital Asset Management 107,
     121
JSR170 31

K
knowledge management (KM) 18, 22

L
learning content management systems
     (LCMS) 22
licenses/agreements management (B2B) 97
lightweight directory access protocol
     (LDCAP) 43
linear planning 10

manipulation tools 45
marketing automation 22
marketing content management (MCM)
     21–22
M
Martha Stewart Omnimedia xiv
media asset management (MAM) 21
media enterprise application suite xi
metadata 15, 39, 52, 108, 121, 133
   access control 133
   application security 133
   administrative interfaces 128–129
   building templates 122
   definition 108, 121
   editing interfaces 128
   hierarchical composition 122
   hierarchies 131
   information display interfaces 128
   metadata-driven security 44
   model 9
   relationship index 22
   search interfaces 128
   structure 108
   testing 132
Microsoft xv, 102, 129
Microsoft.NET xv, 103
Microsoft Active Directory 43, 129
Microsoft Internet Explorer xv, 95

Microsoft Media Player 50
Microsoft Office 100
Microsoft Word 92
multilanguage display 118
multiple protocol label switching (MPLS) 95

N
n-tier back end architecture 85–86
National Contract Management Association
     48
network 94
   multiple protocol label switching
     (MPLS) 95
   network security 95
     encryption (SSL) 95
     virtual private networks (VPN) 95
   network speed or bandwidth 94
Northplain 114
notification 45

O
object 108
   definition 108
object management group (OMG) 105
object-oriented (OO) programming 104
ontology 109
   definition 109
open architecture 29
open standards 29, 41, 84, 105
optical character recognition (OCR) 24, 84

P
parallel structures 88, 113, 117
parallel workflow 45
parent/child relationship 109, 126
   definition 109
peripheral tools 23, 27, 83, 92
   desktop application plug-ins 92
   server-based media preparation, transfor-
     mation, and indexing tools 92
pharmaceutical industry xiv, 1
phased methodology 39
phased project management 7
Plone xv, 30, 91
podcasting xiv
programming environments/language 103
   Java 2 Platform Enterprise Edition (Java
     EE) 103
   Microsoft.NET 103
   Perl 104
   Python 104
project management 7, 9, 71–75, 82
polyhierarchical taxonomies 113, 116

protocols and communications standards 104
common object request broker architecture (CORBA) 105
Java community process (JCP) 106
Java database connectivity (JDBC) 106
Java remote method invocation API (RMI) JSR-170 106
object management group (OMG) 105
remote procedure call (RPC) 104
simple object access protocol (SOAP) 104

Q
QuarkXPress xv, 25–26, 38, 92, 99, 125, 131, 133
Quark Production System for newspapers (QPS)

R
Rafael Ltd. 18
case study 18
rapid application development (RAD) 103
records management (RM) 1, 21, 24, 28, 52
remote procedure call (RPC) 104
return on investment (ROI) xiv, 2, 20, 57, 67, 89
calculating ROI 67
intangible return 79
brand compliance 80
improved communications 80
improved competitive position 80
improved staff awareness of company IP 81
increased number of use and reuse of IP 81
legal compliance 80
internal rate of return (IRR) 68
methods 67
activity-task based, bottom-up model 68, 138
bottom down 140
hybrid approach 69
top-down, traditional ROI calculation 69
models 67
net present value (NPV) 68

role of ROI 71
calculating initial costs 72
cost of ownership 76
intangible costs
investment 71
ongoing costs 73
tangible return 76
savings from expedited time to market 77
savings from gained productivity 76
saving in shipping and handling costs 79
total cost of ownership (TCO) 68
rich media file management 37
rich media management 1, 80
rich media file xi, 37
rich media management systems 80

S
Safari xv, 95
Sarbanes-Oxley law (SOX) 51–52, 59–60
saved searches 44, 128
scheduling 45
search engine 23
security logic 23
serial workflow 45
service oriented architecture (SOA) 30, 85, 102
definition 102
simple object access protocol (SOAP) 100, 104
software development kit (SDK) 103
storage/archiving 93
distributed storage 94
near-line 93
off-line 93
online 93
structured content 37–38
structured versus unstructured content 37–38
supply chain management 97
system architecture 41, 85, 96
system security 34, 41
application security versus UI filters 42
authentication 43
intersecting permissions 42
lightweight directory access protocol (LDAP) 42
metadata-driven security 44
privileges and permissions 42
single sign on (SSO) 43

T

taxonomy 5, 6, 39, 107
   advanced 107
   building the taxonomy or hierarchical
        structure 109
   classification tree 111
   content map 110
   definition 107
   hierarchical structure 109
   identify non-unique labels 111
   management tools 115, 119
   model 9
   short-term vs. long-term 111
   synonyms 112
   unique code 111
Telescope 114
text-based document xi, 1, 23
threads 52

U

unstructured content 37–38
   structured versus unstructured content
        37–38
usage rights restriction 47–50
   sample rights matrix 49
   tracking 48, 50
use and user data aggregation 97
use cases for user groups and roles 34
   template 36
user feedback 3–4, 9–10, 27
user interface (UI) 40
   desktop clients 95
      browser-based 95
      thick clients 96
      thin clients 95
   requirements 40

V

versioning 33, 52, 106, 131, 136
version tracking 52

W

web content management xi, 1, 21, 28, 30,
        38, 116
workflow 44–45
   tracking and reporting 45
work flow engine 23
write once ready many (WORM) devices
        24, 52

X

XML 38, 51, 100, 104

Z

Zweites Deutsches Fernsehen (ZDF) 4
   case study 4